Science
Business

Science
Business

THE PROMISE,
THE REALITY,
AND THE FUTURE
OF BIOTECH

Gary P. Pisano

HARVARD BUSINESS SCHOOL PRESS
Boston, Massachusetts

Library of Congress Cataloging-in-Publication Data

Pisano, Gary P.
    Science business : the promise, the reality, and the future of biotech /
Gary P. Pisano.
        p. cm.
    ISBN 1-59139-840-1
 1. Biotechnology industries—History. I. Title.
    HD9999.B442P57 2006
    338.4'76606—dc22

                                                              2006016541

To my father,

Daniel J. Pisano

Contents

Preface

The Rise of a New Industry, and a Big Question

The journey behind this book began more than twenty-one years ago, when as a doctoral student at the University of California, Berkeley, I stumbled upon the then-infant biotechnology industry. It was 1985, just a couple of years after the first wave of initial public offerings of young biotechnology firms like Genentech, Cetus, Chiron, Biogen, and Amgen. A number of things intrigued me about the industry. First, it was cauldron of experimentation and innovation in the organization of R&D. Unlike traditional pharmaceutical R&D, biotechnology R&D was largely being organized through a web of collaborative arrangements between large, established pharmaceutical companies and entrepreneurial entrants. At the time, such alliances were not as common as they are today across industries, and there was a sense that biotechnology was at the vanguard of a new and better way of organizing R&D. Second, this was an industry where private firms were essentially conducting what could normally be considered fairly basic science. There really was not much precedent in other industries for the degree to which science and business were converging. Finally, I was struck by the optimism of those involved in this fledgling sector, who hoped to transform not just the pharmaceutical industry, but also human health in

ix

general. Many observers at the time expected the industry to follow a
similar path to that of semiconductors, where the advent of solid-
state technology not only led to dramatic improvements in products,
but also fundamentally reshaped the competitive landscape.

Over much of the next two decades, my interest (some of my colleagues would say my obsession) with biotechnology and the pharmaceutical industry only grew. I researched collaborative arrangements
and new organizational forms, studied the factors affecting development performance, and wrote numerous case studies on biotechnology and pharmaceutical companies' strategies. I also consulted for
numerous companies in this sector. The scientists and executives I
met and worked with in this industry were among the smartest, most
dedicated, and most imaginative people I had ever known. The sector
seemed to have little trouble convincing others (and particularly
investors) of its bright prospects. Virtually every industry conference
(year after year) was full of sunny prognostications. Everything we
knew about business and industry performance indeed suggested a
very promising future for biotechnology, not just commercially but
also for its ability to transform drug therapy.

And yet, as the years passed, I became increasingly puzzled by
something. My sense was that things were not working as well as
expected. I found this troubling because without a healthy biotechnology sector, I believed, the great promise of biotech to impact
human health would go largely unrealized. I assembled data on the
financial performance of all publicly held biotechnology firms and
rolled up an aggregate income statement (in essence, treating the
industry as if it were one firm). I plotted this over twenty years and
found that while revenues grew exponentially over time (as might be
expected for an emerging industry), operating income (before depreciation) was essentially zero or slightly negative in most years. Once I
took the industry's dominant firm—Amgen—out of the sample, the
picture got bleaker. The industry, in aggregate, had lost money over its
life span. And these were just the *publicly* held companies, which
were supposed to be in better shape than the hundreds of private
companies, all of which almost certainly lost money. I report this data
analysis in this book, along with other figures supporting the disappointing financial returns of the sector.

Another surprise concerned the R&D performance of biotechnology firms. One of the assumptions of biotechnology is that it would lead to significant improvements in drug R&D productivity. Biotechnology firms were supposed to be much more efficient at pharmaceutical R&D because they were both on the cutting edge of science and unencumbered by the bureaucracy and organizational inertia of the behemoth pharmaceutical companies. However, to my knowledge, this presumption had never been tested with data. I therefore assembled an extensive data set of R&D and drug launches of both biotechnology companies and established pharmaceutical companies (for details, see chapter 6) and conducted a productivity analysis that spanned close to twenty years. What I found was again surprising: there was no discernable difference in the R&D productivity of biotechnology firms (in aggregate) and large pharmaceutical firms. Thus this sector was not only experiencing disappointing financial results, but it was also failing to stand out even where it was clearly supposed to have an advantage. The promise of biotechnology was not reflected in the reality.

This book explores the nature and causes of this gulf between the promise and reality of biotechnology. Why, after thirty years, has this sector not performed up to expectations? Critics might argue that thirty years is not enough time to measure the performance of an industry and that the payoffs are just over the horizon. I contemplated this line of reasoning for some time. However, it troubled me that such predictions of imminent prosperity and productivity have been made in biotechnology since the dawn of the sector. Furthermore, as I looked more deeply into the sector, I came to realize that the problems of the sector were *structural* in nature and that time would not solve the problem. The framework I develop in this book is fairly straightforward. I argue that the performance of a science-based business, like biotechnology, hinges on how well the sector is organized and managed to deal with the fundamental business problems created by science. Thus I start with the science. The sciences behind biotechnology create a very specific set of "functional requirements" for the business. These are *risk management, integration,* and *learning.* The question is, How well is the sector set up to deal with these three problems?

My analysis reveals that the biotechnology sector is not structured in a way that enables it to deal very well with these three problems. A strong focus on monetizing intellectual property has impeded flows of information, led to fragmentation, and created a proliferation of new firms. As I discuss in this book, these three characteristics work directly against the requirements of risk management, integration, and learning at the organizational level. The root cause behind this mismatch is that the sector has indiscriminately borrowed business models, organizational strategies, and approaches from other high-technology industries under the (false) premise that if it worked there it will work here. Not all high-technology industries are alike, and science-based businesses like biotech have unique challenges and thus call for different approaches. Highlighting these differences and understanding their implications for business strategies and models, organizational structures, and institutional arrangements is one of the chief missions of this book.

A more fundamental issue explored is the relationship between business and science. Traditionally, these two pursuits lived in different spheres. The university was the bastion of science; the for-profit enterprise, the keeper of business. The distinction, of course, has not always been perfectly clear. Some great scientists were entrepreneurs, and some large corporations (e.g., IBM, GE, AT&T, Xerox) were home to extraordinary basic research laboratories. But by and large the science/university and business/private enterprise distinction was a reasonably accurate description of the prevailing "division of labor" for the vast majority of industries throughout the twentieth century. In biotechnology, these two worlds began to converge. Private firms undertook research projects that only a few years earlier would have been the sole purview of a university laboratory. At most, the science behind the companies was so new—so raw—it would require years of further validation. Some early-stage biotech companies shared laboratory space (and staff) with universities or academic hospitals. In my parlance, a "science-based" business is one that is not just a passive user of science, but also an active participant in the process of advancing science either directly (through in-house research) or indirectly (through sponsored research). From the other side, universities clearly began to see their science as a business. They aggressively patented and sought licensing deals, collaborated with venture capitalists to launch firms, and even began to move downstream into drug development. Both private enterprises and universities were in the business of science. This fact leads to a deeper question that I explore in this book: Can science be a business?

The increasingly close relationship between business and science is a subject that has drawn extensive attention both in academic writing and the popular press. The focus of these writings is generally on the potential deleterious effects this relationship can have on scientific research. This is a complex and important set of issues. My angle is somewhat different. I look at the problem from the perspective of business. What happens to business performance (profitability, productivity, etc.) when businesses become involved in science either directly or indirectly? An exploration of the thirty-year experiment known as the biotechnology sector provides some clues to answering this question. This book represents my attempt to extract these clues and to provide some insights that might be useful to managers and investors in the biotechnology and pharmaceutical sectors and scholars and practitioners interested in the science-business relationship more broadly.

While this book delves into biotechnology and pharmaceuticals in depth. I hope that more general messages can be extracted that have relevance well beyond this sector. Let me preview three of these.

First, the nature of science matters to the appropriate design of business models, organizational structures, and institutional arrangements. One should always be on the lookout for what can be leveraged from the experiences of other sectors, but such borrowing cannot be done indiscriminately. What may have worked in one sector may not work in another because differences in the underlying scientific landscape create focal problems for business to solve. Science-based businesses involve unique challenges based on the nature of science that "stress" traditional business models, approaches, and arrangements. While entire sectors cannot be designed, they have designs. In this book, I refer to the design of the sector as its "anatomy." A match between the anatomy of the sector and the nature of the science is a prerequisite for long-term performance.

Second, and clearly related to the above, all business practices, models, and arrangements involve trade-offs. There are few universally best practices that work everywhere independent of context. For instance, entrepreneurial models solve one set of problems (managing risk) but can create others (loss of integration). The same can be said of large, vertically integrated enterprises, university licensing, venture capital, and other a host of other arrangements. Too often a particular business form or model is anointed to become dominant based on what it does particularly well, without thinking through its inevitable weaknesses.

Finally, in the context of science-based business, we are still very much in the learning phase. Experimentation and innovation in business models, structures, and arrangements are as important to the health of these sectors as the experimentation and innovation in the science. All major epochs of technological changes have involved not just innovation in technology, but also innovation in businesses. The "invention" of large-scale integrated enterprises (in the late nineteenth century), multinational corporations (in the mid-twentieth century), and entrepreneurial enterprises (in the mid- to late twentieth century) are excellent examples of how business innovations transform industries. The science-based business is potentially just such an innovation that will fundamentally influence economic growth in the twenty-first century.

A book like this would simply not have been possible without the help and support of many dedicated people and organizations. I would first like to thank Kim Clark (retired dean) and Jay Light (current dean) of the Harvard Business School for their encouragement and support of my work. I could not have completed this book without some very important steps they each took to help me. I am also grateful to Jean Cunningham, Assistant Dean, Administration and Educational Affairs, at the Harvard Business School for helping to clear some obstacles that could have derailed this project. I am also sincerely grateful to the Harvard Business School Division of Faculty Research and Development for generously funding my research and to my research directors over the course of this project (Krishna Palepu, Ananth Raman, and Marco Iansiti) for their support.

I was blessed with an incredibly talented and dedicated research team. I would like to thank Barbara Feinberg, who consulted with me throughout this project right from the very inception more than five years ago. She helped me formulate the ideas and form them into a book. She also provided a continuous flow of extraordinarily helpful feedback on numerous written drafts. Clarissa Ceruti provided invaluable assistance on the chapters involving the science of biotechnology. I am also indebted to Chris Allen for his excellent support of the data analyses. Eli Strick, who worked with me for two years on the book, was tenacious in hunting down and analyzing hard-to-find data. I am grateful not just for his dedication during his time at Harvard Business School, but also for his willingness to help out on weekends long after he had left the school. I would like to thank Sharon Pick, who worked as my consulting editor during the writing of the manuscript. She not only did a wonderful job making sure the prose flowed, but her ten years of experience in the biotechnology industry made her an invaluable sounding board for many of the ideas presented in the book. I am deeply indebted to Francesco Gino, my postdoctoral fellow at Harvard Business School during the past two years. As my research collaborator, she shaped my thinking about many of the core issues I confronted in the book. I am grateful for the incredibly long hours she invested to bring this manuscript to life.

I would like to thank the following people, who read drafts of the manuscript and provided extremely helpful comments: Kent Bowen, Bill Sahlman, Ed Scolnick, Richard Nelson, and David Scharfstein. I was also fortunate to benefit from discussions about the issues contained in the book with John Rehr, Vicki Sato, Robert Huckman, Lee Fleming, Jonathan West, Srikant Datar, and Michael Tushman. I thank Jeff Kehoe, my editor at Harvard Business School Press, for his support, encouragement, and patience on a project that took somewhat longer than expected. I would also like to thank Dino Malvone and Sarah Castonguay for the final preparation of the manuscript.

This is usually the part of a preface where the authors thank their families for providing the peace and tranquility needed to write the book. With two highly spirited teenagers at home, I am not sure the words "peace" and "tranquility" are the first two that come to mind. Nevertheless, I am grateful to my family for their support and for the distractions they provided that kept my mind focused on the issues that matter.

There is one person I would very much wish to thank in person but I cannot. My father, Daniel Pisano, who passed away earlier this year, was a truly remarkable man who had a hand in every accomplishment of my life, including this effort. It is to him I dedicate this book.

1

The Science-Based Business

A Novel Experiment

For more than twenty-five years, the biotechnology industry has been host to a profound and important experiment: the fusion of science and business. Perhaps in no other industry have science and business been as tightly interwoven as they have become in biotechnology. Over the past century, of course, science has played a critical role in a number of industries (e.g., semiconductors, computers, advanced materials). But it remained *outside* the boundaries of the business system. Science was a tool, an input, or a foundation for creating new products and services; it was not the business. From its conception, biotechnology was different. In biotechnology, the science *is* the business. That was true in 1976, when Genentech, the first biotechnology firm, was founded by a venture capitalist and a Nobel Prize–winning scientist. It remains true today, as universities ally with venture capitalists to develop new drugs. The history of the biotechnology industry provides a fascinating view of this convergence of two previously distinct realms—science and business.

1

The significant challenges of integrating science and business have driven this sector to pursue novel organizational and institutional experiments that encompass various forms of collaboration between firms, business models for capturing value from innovation, definitions of what constitutes intellectual property, contractual arrangements used to "monetize" intellectual property, the "rules" by which academic institutions and private companies interact, and the boundaries delineating private versus government research. The history of biotechnology thus provides a rich opportunity—a laboratory, some might say—to examine the more general challenges of running a science-based business. Providing an in-depth understanding of these challenges, and strategies for dealing with them, is the focus of this book.

THE SCIENCE-BASED BUSINESS

To understand the challenges of a science-based business, we must first answer a basic question: what is a science-based business? Specifically, what is distinctive about such a business? Of course, many firms and industries (e.g., semiconductor, electronics, communications, advanced materials) use scientific knowledge to create innovative products and solutions. The *use* of science, however, does not in and of itself define a science-based business. In this book, the term *science-based* is used to connote a commercial enterprise or collection of enterprises that attempts to both create science and to capture value from it. That is, the science-based business actively participates in the process of advancing and creating science. Moreover, a significant part of the economic value of the enterprise is ultimately determined by the quality of the science upon which it rests.

Biotechnology is a science-based business. There are notable examples of private enterprises—both large and small—contributing directly to the advancement of basic biomedical science. For instance, upon its founding in 1976, Genentech's research focused on resolving basic scientific issues of cloning genes and expressing proteins in bacteria cells. Kary Mullis, a scientist employed at Chiron, invented polymerase chain reaction, one of the most important techniques for undertaking genetics research—and an invention for which he won a Nobel Prize. A private company, Celera, competed against a massive government-sponsored initiative to sequence the human genome. Scientists at Merck were the first to identify the structure of the virus that causes AIDS.

Of course, these landmark examples are rare. It is more common for firms to engage in research where the science is still "raw," the data are mixed, and basic technical feasibility remains in doubt. Consider the example of RNA-interference (RNAi), a major advance in our understanding of how to selectively "switch off" genes (by interfering with the process by which RNA translates DNA into specific proteins). Within months of the publication of key articles on RNAi in the leading scientific journals, several firms were founded to use the technique to attempt to discover drugs. A similar pattern can be found in genomics, stem cells, systems biology, and proteomics—all were new streams of science that attracted significant commercial investment long before the science was fully worked out. By necessity, firms involved in such areas were forced to participate in resolving basic scientific questions and in establishing proof of feasibility through either their own R&D or through collaboration with university scientists. The close links between private enterprise and universities show up in data on scientific publications and in particular in the amount of collaboration between corporate and academic scientists.

While private companies have become more involved with basic science, universities and academic medical centers have become more involved in the business aspects of their science. Virtually all major research universities and teaching hospitals have industrial liaison and technology licensing operations to both bring in research funding and to appropriate returns on intellectual property. The financial stakes are not trivial. It has been estimated, for example, that Columbia University's patents on basic recombinant DNA technology (known as the Axel patents) brought the university revenues of $300 million to $400 million over two decades, with more than $100 million in its peak year.[1] The Massachusetts General Hospital, an affiliate of the Harvard Medical School, earned $46 million in licensing revenues in 2003, with about half of this coming from the patents on just one product—the blockbuster biotechnology drug Enbrel.[2] Many universities, including MIT, take equity stakes in new ventures

started by their faculty. Increasingly universities are no longer limiting themselves to the earliest stages of basic biomedical research but
have begun to move "downstream," into the development and testing
of drugs. In short, science has become a business.

It is clear that, at some level, the basic needs of a science-based
business are no different from those of any other business. Organizations need to secure capital. Scarce resources (human, financial,
intellectual, etc.) have to be allocated to projects with uncertain payoffs. Assets need to be valued and managed. Contracts with various
partners must be designed and executed. Advanced economies
already have existing institutional and organizational arrangements to
carry out these functions (e.g., capital markets, venture capital, contracts, intellectual property, corporate organizations). Furthermore,
an entire set of management practices, principles, and tools—what I
call "management technology"—are available to operate businesses.
In general, these arrangements and technologies have evolved over
centuries and work quite well for most of the economy. The basic thesis of this book, however, is that a science-based business entails
unique challenges that require different kinds of organizational and
institutional arrangements and different approaches to management.
Posed simply, what works well in other settings may not work as well
in a science-based setting.

THE BIOTECHNOLOGY EXPERIMENT:
TAKING STOCK AFTER THIRTY YEARS

If we identify the birth of the biotechnology industry with the founding of Genentech, the sector is thirty years old. It is fair to ask, How is
the sector doing? There is little doubt that, since the invention of
genetic engineering technology in the early 1970s, we have been living amid one of the greatest scientific revolutions in human history.
By almost any measure—rates of publication, growth of biological
databases, increases in patenting, numbers of landmark scientific discoveries, and so on—there has been a veritable explosion of basic
biomedical know-how. Scientifically, it would be hard to argue that
the life sciences revolution has not been a striking success. Many
both inside and outside the industry—scientists, venture capitalists,

Wall Street analysts, senior executives, policymakers—expected that this scientific revolution would also create enormous financial rewards: the new science would lead to a vast trove of new drugs, and these drugs would create massive economic profits. This is the logic that attracted both private and public equity and enabled the creation of a biotechnology sector.

But how well has this sector performed as a business? While there have been a few very successful biotechnology firms (e.g., Amgen, Genentech, Genzyme), the economic performance of the sector overall has been disappointing by any objective standard. Figure 1-1 shows the total revenues and profitability of all publicly held biotechnology companies (in aggregate) from 1975 to 2004. In

FIGURE 1-1

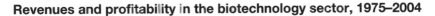

Revenues and profitability in the biotechnology sector, 1975–2004

$ millions

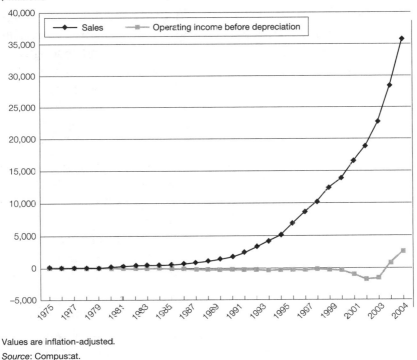

Values are inflation-adjusted.

Source: Compustat.

essence, this figure presents an aggregate income statement of the biotechnology sector as if it had been one firm.

While revenues have grown steadily, profits have hovered consistently at or below zero, according to the most recent data. In later chapters I explore the performance of the sector in depth and from various angles, but the basic conclusion is the same: the vast scientific success has yet to translate into financial success or improved drug R&D productivity. This paradox begs the question, Why is this so?

THE CHALLENGES OF SCIENCE
AS A BUSINESS

The thesis of this book is that the disappointing performance of the biotechnology sector reflects a fundamental and deep struggle between the conflicting objectives and requirements of the *science* of biotechnology and the *business* of biotechnology. Conflicts between science and business—some obvious, some subtle—are apparent at many levels, beginning with their different cultural norms, values, and practices. For example, science holds methodology sacred; business focuses on results. Science values openness and sharing (with attribution); business generally demands secrecy and propriety.[3] Science demands validity (Is this idea/finding valid? Does it stand up to scrutiny?); business demands utility (Is it useful?). Both areas can be fiercely competitive, but they compete for different currency. Science "keeps score" by intellectual impact and contribution to a body of knowledge, as measured by prestige, academic standing, peer evaluation, and published articles; business does so by financial performance. The clash of these norms, values, and practices becomes most apparent when private enterprises and universities collaborate. But they are also lurking for any enterprise engaged in the business of science. Once science becomes a business, there is tension between the criteria required by business institutions (markets) and the criteria used by institutions of science.

As institutions, businesses perform some fairly basic economic functions. They allocate resources (human, financial, intellectual) to investments; they manage risks; they coordinate (through contract and organizational processes, sets of activities and resources to create value; and they appropriate profit streams on behalf of their owners. In advanced economies, a large set of institutional arrangements, rules, and organizational structures and management technologies have evolved to handle these functions. For instance, patents help companies claim rights to the fruits of their R&D investments (appropriability); accounting practices and methods provide us pictures of how well companies are performing financially; capital markets keep score and allocate resources to enterprises; techniques like discounted cash flow and real option valuation help managers allocate resources and manage risks; boards of directors are supposed to ensure that surpluses are appropriated by owners; and contracts coordinate activities among firms and divvy up a value and risks. When needed, specialized arrangements or bodies have emerged to fill "gaps" in existing institutional structures. Thus, for instance, venture capitalists emerged to fill a "void" in the capital markets for risky, early-stage ventures.

Science-based businesses are challenged by the characteristics of science that "stress" these institutional arrangements, rules, organizational technologies, and management practices. In this book, I argue that challenges to the business of biotechnology are rooted in three specific characteristics of the science of biotechnology: (1) the *profound and persistent uncertainty* of the science of biotechnology requires mechanisms for managing and rewarding risk, (2) the highly *complex* and *heterogeneous* nature of the scientific knowledge base requires mechanisms for integration across disciplines and functional areas of expertise, and (3) the rapid cadence of scientific progress requires mechanisms for cumulative learning. The health of the sector depends on how well it can cope with *all three* of these challenges.

Profound and Persistent Uncertainty and Management of Risk

All businesses, from the corner dry cleaners to the global high-tech corporation, must manage risk and uncertainty. By definition, R&D, regardless of the industry, entails risk. But by working at the frontiers of science, a science-based business like biotechnology confronts levels of risk and uncertainty well beyond what is entailed in "normal" R&D. Even in high-tech contexts like semiconductors, high-performance computers, and aircraft, R&D projects, while risky, rest on a foundation of technological feasibility. Existing principles, methods, causal theories, and heuristics evolved from years of experience define an envelope of feasible trajectories for commercial R&D.[4]

In science-based business, R&D confronts fundamental questions about technical feasibility. Is it possible to express a protein in a bacteria cell? Is it possible to culture mammalian cells in vitro? What genes are involved in depression? Which biochemical pathways are involved in inflammation? What role do kinases play in certain diseases? Why are some people more likely than others to be stricken with Alzheimer's disease? These are the types of questions with which science-based businesses in biotechnology have had to grapple.

Not only are such questions difficult to answer, but the attempt to answer them leads, in all likelihood, to more questions—or to unexpected results. Thus the uncertainty faced by science-based business differs in its very nature from that faced by other kinds of business. In 1921 Franklin Knight distinguished between *primary* and *secondary* uncertainty.[5] The latter can be characterized by probability distributions (What is the chance of a freeze in Florida next winter? How likely is it that consumers will prefer green sweaters to blue sweaters next year?). Secondary uncertainty is often referred to as "known unknowns." Primary uncertainty refers to "unknown unknowns": to put it another way, it is everything you did not even know you did not know.

In the context of biotechnology, the challenges of high risk and primary uncertainty are further amplified by the long time horizons over which these risks and uncertainties are resolved. Drilling for oil or making a Hollywood movie is risky. Most oil wells turn out dry and most Hollywood films do poorly at the box office (indeed, most are not even released to theaters but go straight to video or, worse, are shown on long flights!). But discovering that an oil well is dry or that a film is a dud takes a relatively short period of time. In science, however, the uncertainty and risks may linger for years, sometimes decades. Cancer continues to prove a devilishly difficult disease to understand and treat despite several decades of massive investment in basic research.[6] And even when one finds a "solution," it does not necessarily have clear implications for commercial R&D; rather, it may instead trigger a new round of basic research. The successful sequencing of the human genome marked the beginning—not the end—of a process of understanding the role of genetics in disease.

Primary uncertainty that requires long periods of time and heavy R&D investments to resolve means that mechanisms for managing risk and rewarding risk taking are absolutely essential to the science-based business. Such mechanisms include private equity markets and venture capital for channeling resources to entrepreneurial firms, public equity markets to provide liquidity (and thus reward investors for risk), contractual arrangements (e.g., licensing) for allocating rights to intellectual property, and institutional arrangements for protecting and appropriating economic returns from intellectual property (e.g., patents). Together, these mechanisms constitute a strategy for what I call the *monetization of intellectual property*. That is, know-how itself has become a separable asset that is traded, valued, and appropriated As discussed in later chapters, monetization of intellectual property (IP) has been used successfully in many other industry contexts. This book explores how these mechanisms for risk management—and the monetization of IP in particular—have worked in the specific context of biotechnology.

Some very particular challenges of science-based business potentially stress these mechanisms. In order for any asset to be monetized, for instance, one needs to solve the appropriability problem. *Appropriability* is the ability of a firm (and its investors) to capture value from an asset Businesses care about valuation; they care in particular about the value that they can capture (appropriate). The returns from any asset can be roughly divided into two parts: the *private* (or appropriable) returns and the *social* (or nonappropriable) returns. Private returns refer to the economic rents that investors can appropriate for themselves. The social returns refer to the economic benefits that flow to others (customers, suppliers, competitors, workers, and owners of complementary assets). Private returns hinge on one's ability to *exclude* others from accessing an asset without paying for it. To appropriate returns on R&D, businesses generally use such devices as patents, copyrights, and trade secrets.[7] Studies by various researchers show that the effectiveness of such mechanisms varies significantly across technologies and sectors. In general, complete exclusion is quite difficult, and as a result, companies do not appropriate all the returns from their R&D investments. Some returns flow to imitators, for example.

For two reasons, the problems of appropriability grow more complicated for R&D focused on basic science. First, certain types of scientific advances may not fit the criteria for patentability. Or, at the very least, the scope and efficacy of patents in this space may be highly uncertain. (The biotechnology industry, for example, has been a battleground for court challenges on the patentability of a number of basic biological discoveries.) An organization might be able to patent a gene or a protein, but it is currently not possible to patent basic biomedical knowledge. Second, alternative modes of appropriability, such as trade secrets, may be very difficult to implement in the context of scientific norms geared toward publication and dissemination of knowledge. Indeed, when companies enter the business of science, they are generally forced to collaborate with scientists who operate in the academic world. This may raise issues with respect to secrecy and publication. However, increasingly, as academic scientists think about the commercial value of their work, it is not a given that they will share openly. When companies encounter academic scientists who do not share the norm of open science, they may have difficulty getting access to what they might have previously considered "free" science. Companies often lure world-class scientists into in-house research departments, often with the implicit promise of continued ability (if not freedom) to publish. These collaborative and employment relationships must reconcile the conflicting norms of science (publish, disseminate) and of business (keep secret, appropriate).

Highly Complex and Heterogeneous Knowledge and the Problem of Integration

The advances in biomedical sciences over the past thirty years are often characterized in terms of *a* scientific revolution. One often hears the terms "molecular biology revolution," "life sciences revolution," or "genomics revolution" to describe this enormous scientific progress. While such terms are efficient shorthand (indeed, in this book I use similar shorthand), they obscure an extremely important fact: the scientific progress potentially transforming drug R&D and health care is broad-based and cuts a swath across a very wide range of scientific disciplines. Indeed, as discussed more fully in subsequent chapters, it is perhaps best to think about biotechnology as composed of a constellation of scientific revolutions that encompass various fields of biology, biochemistry, chemistry, computer science and bioinformatics, mathematics, physics, engineering, and, of course, various fields of medical science (e.g., immunology, oncology).

The tool kit of drug R&D has become not only much larger in the past thirty years, but also vastly more diverse. Whereas the world of drug R&D was largely one of medicinal chemistry thirty years ago, today it comprises molecular biology, cell biology, genetics, bioinformatics, computational chemistry, protein chemistry, combinatorial chemistry, genetic engineering, high throughput screening, and many other fields. New tools are opening up vast new opportunities, but herein lies a critical challenge. Each tool sheds light on a piece of a very complex puzzle: effectively discovering and developing drugs requires that all the pieces come together. Thus integration across disparate scientific fields, approaches, and functional skill sets is now perhaps more important than ever if the scientific promise is to realize its potential in the form of new drugs and therapies.

Integration is not a challenge unique to drugs. Many other products are the result of integration across fields. Consider the modern jetliner, an enormously complex system whose hundreds of parts must be precisely engineered and manufactured to work seamlessly together. Yet one of the specific challenges created by integration in biotechnology is that the various subfields that need to be integrated are themselves rapidly evolving and highly immature. Thus integration dynamics are quite different. Whereas many complex systems can be decomposed into modular parts with well-defined interfaces that enable specialists to focus on different components, biological science is not yet at the point where it can be modularized. I explore this theme and its important implications for the organization of innovation in the industry in more detail in later chapters. Biotechnology's complex integration dynamics suggest that the sector needs mechanisms to bring specialists from different disciplines together and to facilitate the flow of information across organizational and disciplinary boundaries. This book explores what these mechanisms might look like and in particular whether or not they are consistent with the strategies of IP monetization used to manage risk.

Rapid Cadence of Advance and the Need for Cumulative Learning

The importance of learning and learning organizations has become almost a truism in modern management theories. Skeptics may caution that enthusiasm for organizational learning is often overblown. After all, in some contexts, execution of what is already known may be far more important to success than experimenting with new approaches. However, it is hard to overstate the importance of learning to the long-term health of science-based sectors. The profound and persistent uncertainty we discussed above means that "what is already known" pales in comparison to the possibilities. The rapid pace of scientific knowledge means that new things must be constantly evaluated; decisions must be made about which options to pursue and which to discard. Furthermore, these decisions must be made in the fog of limited knowledge and experience. Mistakes are common, not because people or firms are incompetent, but because they are constantly dancing on the edge of knowledge. The drug industry is a great example of this. The vast majority of attempts to develop new drugs fail, as they show themselves to be unsafe or ineffective.

When failure is far more common than success, learning from failure is a key to making progress. Yet what does it mean to learn from failure, and what are the mechanisms for doing so? Learning can occur at multiple levels in a system (or industry). Individuals can and do learn. A scientist who has spent thirty years doing research on cell growth factors, having done countless successful and unsuccessful experiments, will have presumably accumulated quite a lot of new knowledge from his or her work. Learning can and does also occur at the organizational level. That lab (whether in academia or a company) that this scientist has been part of will have collectively learned many new things from the work of the other people in the lab. And this learning will not just be the aggregate sum of the learning of the individuals in the organization but will be embodied in deeper shared insights of members of the organizational community. Some of this will be formalized in procedures and methods that become part of the operations of the organization, but much will likely also be tacit (but no less important). Differences in rates of organizational learning have been well documented empirically[8] and help to explain why companies that apparently have access to similar human and physical resources seem to have performed so differently (e.g., General Motors versus Toyota). Learning can also occur "above" the level of individual organizations, through broadly diffused knowledge that becomes widely shared among industry participants, such as investors.

One of the questions to be explored in later chapters is the locus of learning in biotechnology. Clearly individual participants in the industry (scientists, managers, investors) have learned, but does learning take place at the organizational or industry level? And does the locus of learning matter to performance? I argue that in a highly turbulent and rapidly evolving context like biotechnology, organizational learning matters. It is not enough for every individual to become "wiser through experience." Because of the challenges of integration discussed above, firms play a critical role as "keepers" of both technical and organizational knowledge. Such organizational learning, however, may be impeded by the very mechanisms that are needed to manage and reward risks.

CONCEPTUAL FRAMEWORK

A recurrent theme in this book is that while the advancement of science is hard, the challenges of managing the business of science may be even more difficult. In many respects, we are in uncharted waters from a management and business point of view. The vast majority of our stock of knowledge about business (e.g., management techniques, business models and strategies, institutional and contractual arrangements, how markets work) flows from experience accumulated in very different technological contexts. The management challenges of the science-based business are novel and as such cannot be addressed with indiscriminate borrowing of practices, models, approaches, and arrangements that have worked well in other industries, including high-tech industries.

The fit between the science and the business matters. To explore this fit, we need to probe in depth the science and its requirements and the strategies used by business to meet the organizational and economic challenges created by the nature of the science (that is, management of risk, integration, and learning). The high-level framework used to organize the discussion in the book is presented in figure 1-2. This framework highlights the interactions among multiple levels of analysis. I contend that the performance of the sector is influenced strongly by how well the business is able to cope with the fundamental challenges created by the science. This analysis takes us on a journey that parallels this framework. The framing question for the analysis is, If one could design this sector from scratch, what would it be designed to do particularly well? This is clearly a hypothetical question. Business sectors (at least outside of centrally planned economies) cannot be designed. Nor, thirty years after the birth of biotech, does it make much sense to talk about starting from scratch. Nevertheless, the question focuses our attention on the notion that all business sectors—biotechnology included—evolve in

FIGURE 1-2

Conceptual framework

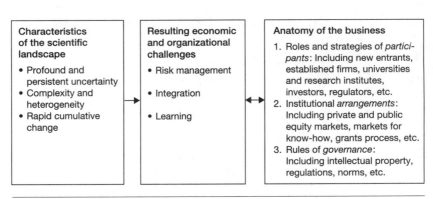

ways to cope with specific types of economic, technological, and environmental challenges.

Sectors cannot be designed by anyone; nevertheless, they do have what we call an *anatomy*. The anatomy of a sector refers to the roles of various types of players (new entrants, established firms, universities, etc.) and their strategies; the institutional arrangements, such as markets for capital, labor, and know-how that link these various players together; and rules of engagement, composed of regulations and norms that shape behaviors and interactions. In this book I probe the evolving anatomy of the biotechnology sector with a view to assessing whether it is suited to solving the fundamental problems created by the scientific environment.

In chapters 2, 3, and 4, I explore the characteristics of the science of biotechnology and the science of drug R&D, arguing that the critical characteristics of the scientific landscape (uncertainty, heterogeneity, and rapid change) have important implications for the problems that businesses in this space must solve. Uncertainty drives the need for risk management; heterogeneity calls for integration; and rapid advance has implications for organizational learning. At the end of chapter 4, I suggest that if one could design this sector, it should be designed to perform risk management, integration, and learning exceptionally well.

Part II (chapters 5, 6, and 7) explores whether in fact the sector is organized (i.e., has the "right anatomy") to address these challenges. Chapter 5 provides an in-depth analysis of anatomy of the sector. Chapter 6 examines the performance of the sector over thirty years, presenting unique data on financial returns, profitability, and R&D productivity. Chapter 7 argues that the disappointing performance of the sector is partially a result of the lack of "fit" between the anatomy of the sector and the requirements of the science. While certain aspects of the anatomy of the sector appear very much aligned with the needs of the science (e.g., managing risk and rewarding risk taking through entrepreneurial business models), less emphasis appears to be given to integration and learning. Thus while models borrowed from other sectors have solved one piece of the biotech business puzzle (risk), they have not done much (and potentially inhibited) the sector's ability to achieve requisite levels of integration and learning.

Part III (chapters 8 and 9) complements the foregoing chapters with a discussion of the implications for business strategies and models (including alliance and licensing strategies) of business firms, the implications for university research and the funding of such research, and potential future scenarios.

TERMINOLOGY AND SCOPE

The term *biotechnology* as used in this book encompasses the broad range of technologies for drug R&D based on scientific advances in such fields as biology, chemistry, medicine, and computer science. This definition is broader than the view of biotechnology as genetic engineering or genomics or biologically produced drugs. I have opted for this broad perspective intentionally to enable an exploration of issues of integration across scientific fields. At the same time, the scope will be restricted to looking at how this scientific revolution has played out in the application to health care– and pharmaceutical-related R&D. I will not be considering applications of biotechnology to agriculture or industrial production.

From an industry perspective, I define a biotechnology firm as any firm founded after 1976 for the purposes of advancing, developing, or commercializing the above new technologies for drug discovery. Historically, "biotech firms" have been distinguished from "pharmaceutical companies" by their technology focus. Biotech firms pursued the novel biological approaches to drug discovery that emerged in the mid-1970s; they sought to create drugs from recombinant and other biological methods. Pharmaceutical companies, in contrast, used the traditional technology of drug discovery—synthetic chemistry. Over time, this distinction has steadily eroded. Established firms have embraced biological approaches, including genomics, to drug discovery, while "biotech firms" employ chemistry. Established pharmaceutical firms—companies like Merck, Pfizer, Novartis, Glaxo, Eli Lilly, and other multinationals—fall very much in the purview of this book. They are players in this space to the extent that they invest through both in-house and collaborative means in novel science for drug R&D. From a technological perspective, both large pharmaceutical companies and biotech firms are part of the same "ecosystem" of drug R&D.

The biotechnology (and pharmaceutical) sector is broad and complex, and my discussion here is necessarily limited in scope. There are vast topics affecting the progress of science and the performance of this sector. Public policy and regulation play huge roles. An entire volume could be written solely on the effects of regulation on this sector (and contribute to the endless debate on whether this sector is over- or underregulated). Regulatory issues are considered only briefly in this book, not because they are unimportant, but, on the contrary, their importance requires depth of analysis that goes well beyond the scope of this book. I take an agnostic view on regulation: it is neither good nor bad, but simply a fact of life in this context that must be considered in any discussion of the industry. I leave it to others to address the complex and important questions related to the appropriateness and effects of these regulations.

LESSONS LEARNED: BIOTECH AND BEYOND

The biotechnology industry offers a rich case history of the interplay and tension between science and business. Through the data and analyses presented, I hope to provide novel insights about how the sector functions, the driving forces that shape how the sector behaves and performs, and potential paths forward. These insights should be of interest to those directly involved in the biotech business (scientists, executives, investors, regulators, and policymakers) and to others who may have an interest in the sector. However, like all case studies, this one is designed to provide insights that may be applicable to related contexts—in this case the relevant application space is science-based business. Businesses based on novel science are likely to play an increasingly important role in the U.S. economy during the current century. Already, a sector based on nanotechnology is beginning to emerge. The United States, with its historically strong research university base, is likely to spawn other science-based sectors. Given the intensifying nature of global competition in high-tech industries from countries like China and India, the ability of the U.S.

economy to foster and sustain such new science-based sectors would seem to be of increasing importance to long-term economic growth. Yet, as suggested by the story of biotechnology, such sectors will require innovation in organizations and institutions to match their technological innovation. Obviously, not all science-based businesses will have the same specific characteristics of biotechnology. Each will have its own unique characteristics and challenges. In grappling with these challenges, leaders of these sectors would be well served by understanding the "lessons learned" from biotechnology experiment.

PART I

THE SCIENCE
OF THE BUSINESS

2

Mapping the Scientific Landscape

This book is about the interaction of science and business—in particular how the nature of science influences the structures, strategies, and institutional arrangements used by business. It thus makes sense to begin with an introduction to the science of discovery. This chapter has two distinct purposes. First, it serves as a primer for those not deeply versed in the science of drug discovery. For readers who have come across, in the popular or business press, terms such as genomics, genetic engineering, and rational drug design without acquiring a deeper understanding of what they actually are, this chapter describes such technologies in a nontechnical way and at a fairly high level of abstraction, explaining how they fit into the broader context of drug science. Second, this chapter describes the scientific landscape in a way that begins to lay the conceptual foundations for subsequent chapters. Too often discussions in both the popular press and academic studies of the pharmaceutical or biotechnology industry treat the science of drug discovery as if it were a single body of knowledge—hence expressions like "*the* life sciences revolution" or "*the* genomics revolution." Such terms obscure the critical fact that not one, but several scientific revolutions have gripped drug discovery. By highlighting the many different areas of the scientific landscape, I hope to convey its inherent complexity and heterogeneity—a fundamental characteristic of the science that I build upon in later chapters.

This chapter has two parts. The first examines drug sciences from a historical perspective, beginning in the late nineteenth century, when researchers first began to identify selective binding of molecular sites with certain chemicals (the origin of the drug target). This history will be helpful in understanding where technology is today and where it may be headed. The second, and more substantial, part describes several of the most important technologies and streams of advance, which can be categorized into three areas: new modes of synthesis, new information about biological mechanisms of disease, and new drug design and screening methodologies.

THE EARLY YEARS OF DRUG SCIENCE— 1870s TO 1930s

Drugs have been used to treat diseases for thousands of years. Since the time of Hippocrates (400 BCE), for example, potions derived from distilled bark and leaves of willow trees have been used to alleviate pain. Despite a long history in the use of drugs as treatments, the modern concept of drug sciences—the discovery or development of drugs based on understanding molecular underpinnings of diseases—dates back only about 125 years. In 1872 Paul Ehrlich, a medical student examining the selective affinity of dyes for biological tissue, hypothesized the existence of "chemoreceptors," molecules that have a selective binding site for chemical agents and mediate specific signaling pathways inside the cell upon binding to the appropriate molecule that activates them.[1] In 1905 J. N. Langley proposed that receptors on cell surfaces served as "switches" that either sent or received biochemical signals. He further hypothesized that desirable therapeutic effects could be achieved by drugs that either blocked or turned on selected "switches." Later research demonstrated that other biochemical switches played a critical role in diseases, including enzymes, ion channels, DNA, and hormones. Ehrlich's and Langley's work defined the fundamental objective for drug discovery that remains current to this day: to find a molecule (a drug) that binds selectively to a target (receptor, enzyme, etc.) in the body to trigger a desired biological effect.

The analogy of "lock and key" is commonly used to describe the action of drugs in the body. One can think of the receptors, enzymes, genes, and hormones as the locks that regulate biochemical processes inside the body. Diseases occur when specific locks are not functioning correctly (or are functioning abnormally) and critical biochemical processes go awry. For instance, cancer results when the processes for triggering normal cell death stop working. In some instances, disease occurs when a specific biochemical lock is produced in excess. For example, high blood pressure results when the body overproduces the enzyme known as angiotensin II. In other cases, disease results from underproduction of a biochemical lock: type I diabetes occurs when the pancreas fails to produce insulin, a hormone needed to metabolize sugar. Drug therapy works in various ways. Some drugs simply replace a lock that is absent (as in the case of insulin therapy for diabetics, or Factor VIII for hemophiliacs). Other drugs act as keys that bind to specific locks, either blocking them (antagonism) or switching them on (agonism). The receptors, enzymes, genes, and other locks that drugs are supposed to interact with are known as targets.

While Ehrlich's and Langley's insights were powerful, drug research was severely handicapped by a lack of analytical tools and biological knowledge needed to identify precisely or characterize the targets and by a lack of knowledge about potential chemicals with therapeutic effects. In short, there were few keys and even fewer locks. Drug discovery in the late nineteenth and early twentieth century thus generally focused on isolating and synthesizing organic compounds from herbs and other natural sources with known or suspected therapeutic properties. For instance, it was not until 1897 that the chemist Felix Hoffmann, in a desperate search for a drug to alleviate his father's suffering from arthritis, was able to extract and synthesize acetylsalicylic acid from the willow tree, creating a pure form of the substance used since antiquity. His employer, Bayer, a dye manufacturer at that time, initially rejected his suggestions to commercialize the drug but eventually decided to produce it, under the name "aspirin."[2]

Ehrlich himself, more than forty years after his pioneering research, went on to discover one of the world's first man-made drugs, salvarsan, a treatment for syphilis. Building on his earlier experiments showing that certain dyes could have antibacterial properties, Ehrlich found salvarsan (derived from arsenic) after synthesizing 606 compounds.[3] Following this successful example, several chemical companies, mostly in Germany and Switzerland, began to systematically isolate active compounds from natural sources such as plants and from coal tar to test their therapeutic potential and to sell them as drugs. Until the 1930s, drug R&D remained a cottage industry at best. Drug companies undertook little scientific research. Harold Clymer, who joined SmithKline as a scientist in 1939, noted: "You can judge the magnitude of [SmithKline's] R&D at the time by the fact that I was told I would have to consider my position temporary since they had already hired two people within the previous year for their laboratory and were not sure that the business would warrant the continued expenditure."[4]

The 1930s saw the rise of more systematic drug discovery, which became organized around the concept of mass random screening. In 1931 Gerhard Domagk, a German chemist at IG Farben, discovered through a mass screening effort in mice that sulfanilamide (a chemical derived from coal tar) had antibacterial effects. Sulfanilamide became the world's first chemically synthesized antibiotic as well as a platform for a class of derivative drugs known as "sulfa drugs." The wartime effort to mass produce penicillin also had a profound impact on drug R&D. Because penicillin and other antibiotics were produced naturally by microorganisms, researchers undertook large-scale sampling of soils, swamps, and other places where microbial life thrived. This approach worked and, as a result, microbial screening became a powerful tool in the search for new drugs during the 1940s. Drug researchers took soil samples from around the world; organic chemists would attempt to isolate and synthesize the organic compounds in these samples. Through this process, companies developed large "libraries" of compounds.

By the 1950s drug R&D scientists had a handle on half of Ehrlich's theory: they could synthesize a reasonably large number of compounds. Unfortunately, knowledge of receptors and the basic biology of diseases remained limited. It was not until 1933, for instance, more than sixty years after Ehrlich first theorized about the existence of chemoreceptors, that scientists discovered the first major enzyme drug target, called carboanhydrase. Experiments demonstrated that sulfa drugs had a diuretic effect by inhibiting carboanhydrase. This led to the development of a class of diuretic drugs known as carboanhydrase inhibitors that were later developed for diabetes, hypertension, and glaucoma.[5] Throughout the postwar era, scientific research in biochemistry led to the identification of a number of important drug targets and therapeutic mechanisms (such as beta-blockers, which block a target on the cell membrane of heart muscle), which in turn led to the discovery and development of important new therapeutics.

But even where target receptors had been identified, the knowledge, methods, and instrumentation needed to find a match between the structure of the receptor and the structure of a chemical drug was completely absent. As a result, drug researchers during most of the twentieth century were forced to rely on random screening of both natural and chemically synthesized compounds against known disease targets. Random screening, in essence, became the first dominant paradigm of drug discovery. Approximately 95 percent of the drugs in use today, in fact, were discovered using this approach.

THE NEW SCIENCE REVOLUTION—
LATE 1970s TO THE PRESENT

Over the past thirty years, advances in molecular and cell biology, genetics, biochemistry, and other disciplines have begun to transform the field of drug R&D through the use of increasingly efficient and sophisticated tools and methods. These advances can be clustered into three broad categories: (1) new modes of synthesis that have expanded the range and type of potential agents that can be used as drugs; (2) new knowledge about the underlying biological mechanisms of disease and the targets for drug discovery; and (3) new design and screening methodologies that have facilitated the search for drugs based on biological information. While cross-cutting technologies have evolved, these broad categories provide a meaningful way to conceptualize the general trends.

New Modes of Synthesis:
Expanding the Range of Therapeutic Agents

Throughout most of the twentieth century, the majority of drugs (or "keys" in this context) that could be synthesized were so-called small molecules.[6] Small molecules are synthesized through methods of organic chemistry, a field that has led to the synthesis of millions of different compounds. However, traditional synthetic chemistry methods are only feasible for making molecules up to a certain size (approximately 500 daltons); there was no generally available method for the large-scale production of nucleic acids and proteins, which are much larger and more complex than traditional small-molecule drugs. Moreover, even small molecules were synthesized in a painstaking process that relied heavily on the hand of the highly skilled chemist.

Since the early 1970s, three new technologies have emerged that greatly expanded both the number and range of compounds that could be synthesized and tested for use as drugs: recombinant DNA, for the production of proteins; hybridization, for the production of monoclonal antibodies; and combinatorial chemistry, for the mass synthesis of large numbers of novel chemical entities. Each of these technologies is described briefly below.

Recombinant DNA. For many years, biomedical researchers hypothesized that proteins might become useful therapeutic agents. Proteins—such as receptors, enzymes, and hormones—play a central role in virtually all biological processes, acting as both locks and keys in a series of biochemical reactions. Some diseases, for instance, occur when the body lacks an ability to produce sufficient quantities of a specific protein. For example, hemophilia is the result of the body's inability to produce sufficient quantities of Factor VIII, an essential clotting factor in human blood. Thus it stands to reason that replacing the missing protein could be an effective way to treat some diseases. Unfortunately, because proteins are very large molecules, they could not be practically synthesized through organic chemical means. Without a means of production, proteins had to be isolated from natural sources, and only a few therapeutic proteins could be obtained: insulin (derived from pig pancreases), human growth hormone (extracted from human cadaver pituitary glands), and Factor VIII (isolated from human blood).

The invention of recombinant DNA (rDNA) techniques changed this. This means of genetic engineering was invented in 1973 by Herbert Boyer and Stanley Cohen.[7] Cohen and Boyer developed a standard protocol for manipulating cells' DNA to induce them to produce a large amount of a specific protein.[8] By using certain biochemical tools, the DNA encoding a particular protein could be isolated and even modified in the desired way. The DNA could then be inserted into a bacterial or mammalian cell, which could be cultured and maintained for purposes of manufacturing the desired protein. Protein excreted from these engineered cells could be isolated and purified.

Recombinant DNA is a good example of a technique that both increases the range of available therapeutics and yet also opens up new avenues for exploring underlying causes of disease. The first uses of rDNA were to produce "therapeutic proteins" (i.e. proteins that could be used as a drug either because the body was not producing enough of the protein on its own or when the protein could be used to stimulate a desired effect).[9] The first therapeutic proteins were substitutes for those that had already been obtained and used from natural sources: insulin, human growth hormone, and Factor VIII were launched in 1982, 1985, and 1992, respectively. Since that time, more than sixty proteins have been developed and commercialized for therapeutic use.

Recombinant DNA was thus initially viewed as a competitive paradigm to synthetic chemistry. At the dawn of the biotechnology industry, certainly many believed that rDNA methods were far superior to organic chemistry for creating drugs. Yet rDNA is a generic technique capable of synthesizing any protein. Since the receptors and enzymes involved in disease processes are also proteins, researchers often use rDNA techniques to synthesize *target* receptors and enzymes that they can use in models aiding the search for potential drugs. Thus rDNA is not always used to synthesize a protein that will be a drug; it is increasingly used to synthesize proteins that are the targets of other drugs. In this way, rDNA has become a complementary method for chemistry-based approaches to drug discovery.

Monoclonal Antibodies. When a "foreign" protein (e.g., a virus or bacteria) enters the body, the immune system automatically triggers the production of *antibodies* that can bind to the invader. Historically, scientists could obtain antibodies only by immunizing an animal with the specific protein against which the antibody was to be generated. The immune system of the animal recognizes the injected molecule as "foreign" and produces antibodies against it. These antibodies are contained in the immune serum, from which the antibody can be isolated and purified. Unfortunately, this technique creates antibodies that react to different parts of the protein, yielding a mixture of antibodies (so called "polyclonal antibodies"). For this reason, its applicability to drug discovery is limited.

In 1975 Georges Köhler and Cesar Milstein invented a technique for producing "monoclonal antibodies" (MAbs).[10] In contrast to polyclonal antibodies, MAbs, characterized by their extremely homogeneous structure, are directed against the exact same part of the target protein.[11] Köhler and Milstein's technique creates an immortal cell by fusing a murine (mouse) myeloma cell with a spleen cell from an immunized animal.[12] The resulting cell can produce virtually unlimited amounts of a particular monoclonal antibody with high specificity for the target protein. MAbs work because diseased cells (e.g., tumor cells) express disease-specific proteins on their membrane surface, some of which represent appropriate targets with which to interact. By interfering with the function of these target proteins, MAbs can influence the course of certain diseases favorably. Because they bind to specific proteins, MAbs can also be used for both in vitro and in vivo diagnostics.

Initially, monoclonal antibodies were developed as vectors for transporting highly toxic drugs used in cancer treatment to proteins specifically expressed by cancer cells so that a minimal dose of the otherwise toxic drug would be sufficient to selectively destroy the diseased cancer cells. During the early 1980s, researchers were hopeful about the use of monoclonals in cancer therapy in particular, but MAbs have also been developed for other conditions, such as septic shock, transplantation, and immunological conditions. Because of their ability to bind selectively to diseased cells, MAbs were often heralded as "magic bullets." Early efforts at developing MAbs for therapeutic use, however, proved to be quite frustrating. Early versions of monoclonal antibodies were derived from murine cells. Unfortunately, when such MAbs were introduced into the human body, they triggered undesired immunological reactions. It was not until scientists discovered techniques to "humanize" MAbs that progress was made in their application to diseases. As of 2002, sixteen MAb-based drugs have been approved by the FDA, and MAbs made up for 25 percent of the biotechnology-derived products in clinical development.[13]

Combinatorial Chemistry. Until fairly recently, medicinal chemists trying to discover therapeutically useful compounds synthesized new molecules one at a time by combining various chemicals and chemical groups. The "art" of medicinal chemistry brought together two bases of knowledge: chemistry—which types of atoms tend to bind to one another, how different chemicals tend to react together, how to break apart a molecule into subgroups, etc.—and medicine—how certain classes of compounds were likely to behave once inside the body. In general, this second body of knowledge was based on empirical experience of which classes of compounds had worked in the past against specific conditions and which had caused undesirable side effects. Over time, this knowledge became more refined.

A big part of the art of medicinal chemistry entailed using a *lead* compound (one that appeared to have some desirable therapeutic effects) to create *analogs* (slightly modified versions) that might offer some combination of greater safety and efficacy. Traditional methods of medicinal chemistry are painstaking, time-consuming, and expensive. For instance, it has been estimated that using traditional synthetic methods, one medical chemist can, on average, produce four compounds per month directed against a particular target for a total cost of about $30,000.[14]

Combinatorial chemistry is an approach to chemical synthesis that produces large numbers of organic compounds by assembling chemical building blocks in every possible combination. Combinatorial chemistry can be traced back to R. Bruce Merrifield's discovery of solid-phase peptide synthesis in the early 1960s, for which he won the Nobel Prize in 1984. Merrifield's techniques enabled peptide chains to be assembled in an automated process. In 1992 Jonathan Ellman reported the first solid-phase synthesis of small organic molecules. The first drugs discovered using combinatorial chemistry entered clinical trials in the early 1990s.

Combinatorial chemistry works on the following principle: any organic molecule can be considered as being composed of two or more chemical groups; by assembling the different combinations, a large number of molecules can be created from a relatively small number of components. If a molecular structure contains, for instance, three structural groups, a robotic chemical synthesizer could prepare $3^3 = 27$ new molecules. This technology also significantly reduces the costs of synthesizing potential therapeutic compounds. Using combinatorial chemistry, 3,300 unique compounds can be produced in one month for a total cost of about $40,000.[15]

The philosophy behind combinatorial chemistry is that by vastly expanding the number of compounds available for testing, researchers can improve the odds of finding a therapeutically useful compound. This is often referred to as increasing the "number of shots on goal." Again, the lock-and-key analogy might be helpful here. Think of a locksmith trying to find a key that fits a certain lock. The locksmith does not know what type or shape of key will fit the lock. Combinatorial chemistry generates lots of random keys that can be tried in the lock.

New Knowledge About Biological Mechanisms of Disease: Expanding Knowledge of Targets

Ever since Ehrlich's theory of chemoreceptors, it has been known that drugs work by interacting with specific cell receptors or enzymes that play a critical role in a disease process. In general, the search for a therapeutically useful compound (be it chemical or biological in origin) is likely to be more productive when the researcher has a known (or at least suspected) target for the drug to interact with. As noted earlier, it was not until the early 1930s that scientists had isolated and characterized the first major drug target (carboanhydrase). Since the dawn of the modern drug research, more than 125 years ago, all the drugs ever introduced have interacted with only about 500 targets.[16] While the exact number of potentially "druggable" targets remains a subject of debate, estimates are in the range of 6,000 to 10,000.[17] Whatever the actual number, our knowledge of locks thus far has been relatively poor.

It is no wonder then that much of the focus of basic biomedical research has been aimed at expanding our knowledge of targets. However, until fairly recently, because the tools and techniques to isolate, identify, and characterize targets were relatively crude, the search for targets was highly iterative, time consuming, and painstaking. In essence, it proceeded with one hypothesized target at a time, and it could take years to fully validate a hypothesis that a specific receptor, enzyme, or hormone played a role in a particular disease. For instance, James Black, one of the greatest drug discoverers of the twentieth century, initiated a research program at Smith Kline in September of 1964 on the role of an unidentified histamine receptor in the secretion of gastric acid (one of the causes of ulcers). It was not until 1970, after synthesizing more than seven hundred compounds, that Black's team was able to confirm in animal studies that there was a second histamine receptor—which they called H2—that played an important role in gastric acid secretion.

The past twenty-five years, however, has seen an explosion in the number of potential targets under investigation for drug research. This progress is due to advances in the tools and techniques for studying disease processes at the cellular and molecular levels that enable researchers to isolate and characterize targets and to dramatic advances in the field of genomics.

Genomics. Genomics is a field of research that examines the DNA sequence and gene functions of different organisms. Today it is increasingly viewed as a way of understanding the underlying (genetic) causes of disease and for illuminating potential biochemical avenues for therapeutic intervention. The idea that genes play a central role in human disease has been around since the dawn of the twentieth century. In 1902 Archibald Garrod, a research physician at St. Bartholomew's Hospital in London, was the first to demonstrate a link between genes and disease while studying alkaptonuria, a rare condition leading to the patient's urine turning black. He found that alkaptonuria was much more likely to afflict people whose parents were blood relatives, and he concluded that the condition was an "inborn error in metabolism."[18]

However, until analytical tools and techniques for isolating, manipulating, amplifying, and characterizing gene sequences were invented, it was impossible to even conceive of studying links between specific genes and specific diseases. This began to change in the mid-1970s, when Fred Sanger invented a technique for "reading" genetic code—or gene sequencing. This gene sequencing enabled scientists to "read" the chemical letters (A [adenosine], T [thymidine], C [cytidine], and G [guanosine]) that make up genes. Initially the process was painstaking and highly labor-intensive, generally involving legions of PhD students laboring over microscopes to analyze the chemical code. Indeed, a PhD itself could be earned by sequencing the genetic codes of a single gene. Craig Venter, who led the private effort to sequence the human genome, recalled that it took him ten years to sequence the gene for the adrenaline receptor.[19]

Then, in the early 1980s, two inventions plowed a path that ultimately led to high-speed automation of sequencing. The first was Kary Mullis's invention of polymerase chain reaction (PCR), a technique for selectively amplifying fragments of DNA that provided a method of producing large quantities of the raw material for genomic studies relatively quickly. The next major step was LeRoy Hood's and Michael Hunkapiller's development of the first analytical instrument that could read genetic code automatically. In 1983 Hunkapiller and Hood formed a new company, Applied Biosystems, to develop and market instruments, reagents, and software used in biotechnology research. In 1986 they introduced the first automated "slab-gel" DNA sequencing system, the 370A DNA Sequencer, capable of analyzing three hundred base pairs per twelve-hour run cycle. Not only did the 370A allow scientists to automate simultaneous testing of DNA, it also digitized the data output from the experiments, facilitating computer analysis of genomic data. By 1995 the 370A's successor, the ABI Prism 377, was capable of reading seventy-two hundred base pairs per hour. Over the next several years, dramatic improvements in the throughput of DNA sequencers made it possible to sequence the entire three billion–element "alphabet" of the human genome in just a few years.

By June 2000 a draft map of the entire human genome had been completed. This was a landmark scientific achievement on the same order as Watson and Crick's double helix. And like Watson and Crick's discovery, the completed map of the human genome marked just a beginning of a new research trajectory. Identifying that a specific strand of DNA represents a gene is helpful, but for it to be useful medically, one needs to understand the functions carried out by that gene: What proteins does it code for? What biological function does that protein play?

In order to be able to study the function of a gene, a scientist must know the gene's location in the genome of the respective organism as well as its sequence. With an increasing number of genome sequences (e.g., human, mouse, fruit fly) available in databases, this task has been greatly facilitated. Scientists can study the function of a specific gene (or groups of genes) in a model organism such as a yeast cell, fruit fly, or mouse by deleting ("knocking out") or modifying the gene and observing the defects that are caused by the omission or modification [20] This information can greatly facilitate the examination of the molecular basis of diseases and the identification of drug targets as well as the prediction of adverse side effects. During this process, the DNA that encodes this particular gene is mixed with different molecules one at a time. Researchers then look for interactions between the DNA and molecules to identify those that influence the function of the gene in the desired way. Research to uncover the functions of genes in this way is called "functional genomics."

Single nucleotide polymorphisms (SNPs, generally pronounced "snips") are often used in this context. SNPs are one-letter variations between different individuals in the sequence of DNA at a given location. If certain sequence variations are known to cause a disease, SNPs can hint an increased risk of developing this disease but most of these variations do not have a deleterious effect. This kind of research is called *structural genomics* since it compares the sequence structure of the DNA of different individuals. It is mostly useful in identifying the molecular roots of diseases (e.g., helping to explain why one person might be more susceptible to diabetes than others).

Genomics has identified a massive number of potential drug targets. The challenge facing researchers today is to validate that those targets have the expected biological effect. For instance, if we took a genomics approach to finding a drug to treat depression, we might begin by trying to identify the genes that affect receptors that play a role in certain neurobiological pathways. However, until there is solid experimental data that those genes really do affect depression, we have so-called unvalidated targets. In many cases, compounds hit a target but do not produce the desired therapeutic effect in an animal or human system. Generally, the process of validating a target takes extensive tissue and animal model studies. The ultimate validation, of course, is proof of efficacy in a human patient.

Further compounding the complexity of the task is the fact that there appear to be relatively few one-gene diseases. That is, most diseases and conditions—including heart disease, type 1 diabetes, Alzheimer's disease, and most cancers—appear to be the result of a complex interaction of multiple genes and the interplay between genes and factors in the environment. Computational methods are now being used to model the interactions of thousands of genes at once with the hope of identifying possible drug targets.

Proteomics. Proteomics is the study of the structure and function of proteins. The task of proteomics is monumental, since the process of translating genetic information from genes into proteins is enormously complex. Although the number of genes in the human genome is large (approximately 25,000 to 35,000), the number of proteins is even larger (between 1 million and 20 million), resulting from different ways in which these genes can be translated. Some genes encode more than one protein, and these proteins are also subject to various forms of modification (such as alternative splicing) before they take on their final biological function. In addition, the examination of proteins is a much more complex task than DNA sequencing. While DNA sequencing has become fully automated, protein sequencing to date still involves a number of manual steps.

The focus of proteomics research is to identify modifications of proteins and eventually to determine how many and which different proteins are derived from each gene in addition to their relative abundance in normal tissue. This protein pattern can then be compared with the protein pattern of diseased tissue by analyzing it to determine the relative abundance, presence, and absence of different proteins. For example, researchers have used proteomics to identify particular proteins associated with atherosclerotic (plaque-coated) arteries as compared to healthy ones. Such information could be used to develop a drug that specifically targets this tissue to prevent the formation of plaque, thus preventing heart attacks, strokes, and hardening of the arteries due to age.

RNA Interference. Until very recently, the targets for drug discovery have either been proteins (receptors, enzymes, etc.) or the genes that code for those proteins. A new technology, known as RNA interference (RNAi), however, has raised the possibility of using RNA as the target for drug intervention. Messenger RNA (mRNA) plays a key intermediate role in the synthesis of proteins. DNA provides the instructions needed for a cell to synthesize a protein. It is the job of mRNA to transcribe that code and carry those instructions to the part of the cell responsible for producing proteins (hence the name "messenger RNA"). The transcription of mRNA from DNA is one of the critical intermediary steps in the biological process by which genes produce proteins. RNAi seeks to find compounds that can interfere with this intermediary process carried out by RNA. In essence, the RNAi makes mRNA another potential target for drug intervention. By selectively interfering with RNA, researchers hope to be able to essentially "switch off" a gene that is expressing a protein that causes some biological problem (e.g., proliferation of cancer cells). RNAi technology is quite recent.[21] The major breakthrough in identifying the genetic mechanisms underlying RNA interference was made in 1998, by Andrew Fire of the Carnegie Institute and Craig Mello of the University of Massachusetts. It was not until 2001 that a research team headed by Thomas Tuschl of the Max Planck Institute isolated the fragments of RNA—small interfering nucleic acids (siNA)—that trigger RNA interference.

Thus RNAi technology encompasses both a novel set of locks (RNA) and a novel set of keys (siNA).

Systems Biology. As noted above, few diseases can be traced to a single "bad" gene. Diseases, and for that matter virtually all biological processes, are manifestations of complex interactions between various biological components (genes, proteins, cells, entire organs). Systems biology is an emerging field that integrates knowledge from genomics, proteomics, cell biology, chemistry, engineering, physics, mathematics, and computer science to study the behavior and performance of complex biological systems. Systems biology clearly builds on the recent advances in genomics and proteomics but shifts the focus of analysis from the level of the component (the individual gene or specific protein) to the level of the biological system (e.g., the cell, the signal pathway across cells) and is deeply concerned with the dynamics of such systems. As Hiroaki Kitano describes in his overview of systems biology in *Science*, "Identifying all the genes and proteins in an organism is like listing all the parts of an airplane. While such provides a catalog of the individual components, by itself it is not sufficient to understand the complexity of the underlying engineered object."[22]

Creating models (based on large data sets from high throughput experimentation) that characterize specific systems is a major focus of systems biology. Researchers hope that such models will enable them to identify specific disease mechanisms that can be the target of drug discovery. Systems biology differs from traditional biology, which is sometimes characterized as "reductionist" or hypothesis-driven in its emphasis on understanding interactions that occur across genes, molecules, cells, and organs. In traditional biology, a scientist starts with a hypothesis about how a specific biologic works (e.g., the role gene X plays in diabetes) and then tests that hypothesis experimentally, with a goal of building an understanding of the system (e.g., the underlying biochemical pathways associated with diabetes) one component at a time. In systems biology, a scientist interested in understanding the genes involved in diabetes might use a gene chip and other analytical instruments to measure the expression of several thousand genes all at the same time. The data from these experiments would then be processed and analyzed using various algorithms to detect which genes are related to others. In terms of applicability to medicinal research, systems biology potentially enables researchers to create models of biochemical pathways associated with specific diseases. These models in turn could provide insights about the disease mechanisms that could be targets for drug discovery.

New Design and Screening Methodologies: Finding Matches Between Locks and Keys

While much has changed over the past 125 years, drug discovery is essentially still a process of finding a match between a drug target of therapeutic interest and a drug compound. The advances described above have vastly expanded our knowledge of potential drug targets and the range and type of drug compounds that can be used against those targets. However, even with advances in knowledge about both compounds and targets, the matching process has, until relatively recently, remained a very labor-intensive, time-consuming process. If one knew the target, then compounds were screened one at a time to find those that bound to it. Over the past fifteen years, two new approaches have evolved that are aimed at improving the ability of researchers to find good matches between compounds and targets: rational drug design and high throughput screening. While these approaches are described separately below, most drug research today combines the two.

Rational Drug Design. Rational drug design (RDD) seeks to "design" therapeutically effective molecules from detailed knowledge of structures and the interaction of the keys and the locks in specific diseases. RDD is a multidisciplinary field that requires contributions from experts in fields such as biochemistry, chemistry, structural studies, chemical synthesis, pharmaceuticals, and computer science.

The goal of RDD is to develop specific drugs based on molecular and structural information as well as biological and chemical functions of target molecules. It is referred to as "rational" because it uses detailed knowledge about diseases, in particular the atomic structure of biologically relevant drug targets, and attempts to build suitable molecules rather than to locate existing ones. Because it requires knowledge about the structure of receptors and enzymes, RDD is also sometimes referred to as *structure-based* drug design. The idea that drug molecules could be designed to treat specific diseases, rather than having to be found, has appealed to drug scientists for many years. Yet without the analytical tools to isolate and characterize drug targets, and to model molecular structures at the atomic level, the approach has been unfeasible.

Rational drug design has been facilitated by advances in a number of technologies. Advances in the set of tools and techniques of genomics, as described above, provide a basis for identifying potential drug targets. The ability to characterize targets at the atomic level has been greatly enhanced through advances in X-ray crystallography and nuclear magnetic resonance spectroscopy. It is now possible for researchers to create highly detailed three-dimensional structural models of complex receptors and enzymes. Computer modeling and simulation of molecules is another improvement that has enabled researchers to design and screen compounds rapidly in silico.

High Throughput Screening. High throughput screening (HTS) is an automated, robotic-based approach for synthesizing and testing many new compounds with a multitude of assays for therapeutic activities against a specific disease. The drug target to be tested is added to a large number of potential drugs in individual wells of a plate by a robot. The robot then performs different experimental procedures and evaluates which of the potential drugs interact with the drug target. Compounds that interact are isolated and subjected to further screening, much of which can again be automated.

HTS can be used with a wide range of possible compounds and targets. The combination of HTS and combinatorial chemistry allows researchers to screen up to 1 million compounds per week, compared to 100 compounds per week 20 years ago. Today many pharmaceutical companies are screening between 100,000 and 300,000 compounds at a time, producing approximately 100 to 300 potential drug candidates, of which only one or two will eventually merit further testing. A technology often used within the HTS process is DNA microarrays, also known as "DNA chips" or "biochips," a powerful tool for screening the possible interaction of keys and locks by using minimal amounts of both compounds.

SUMMARY: CHARACTERISTICS OF THE NEW LANDSCAPE OF DRUG SCIENCE

This chapter was intended to acquaint the reader with various new bodies of knowledge that now underpin the biotechnology revolution and give the reader a feel for the vastness and complexity of the underlying science. A brief history of drug R&D was included in order to provide some perspective on the enormous changes the new scientific advances introduce. Three themes characterize the changes taking place in the scientific landscape of drugs.

First is the dramatic expansion of the landscape for drug development. Whereas the game of drug discovery had historically been played on a fairly constrained grid of small chemical entities and several hundred biological targets, scientific advances have greatly expanded the number and range of potential therapeutic agents (recombinant proteins, antibodies, etc.) and the number of potential targets. Moreover, scientists are now armed with a broader array of tools and techniques for exploring this landscape for attractive matches between drugs and targets. As discussed in subsequent chapters, while this growth of the landscape is good news, it brings with it a new set of organizational challenges related to uncertainty. Formerly, the chief problem a drug R&D organization had to face was opportunity scarcity; increasingly, the problem is one of digesting a diet rich in opportunities, each of which is shrouded in uncertainty.

Second, not only has the landscape grown larger, it has grown more complex and heterogeneous. Whereas thirty years ago drug R&D was largely based on chemistry, today it draws on a broad range of scientific disciplines, tools, and methodologies. Several traditional scientific disciplines have moved to center stage in drug discovery, such as molecular biology, cell biology, and biophysics. Drug research today also draws just as heavily on chemistry, medicine, math, physics, computer science, engineering, and materials science. Moreover, new subfields have emerged that cut across disciplines, including genomics, proteomics, bioinformatics, computational chemistry, computational genomics, chemo-genetics, antibody engineering, protein chemistry, and systems biology.

Again, the growing scientific diversity of the landscape is good news. It has opened up new options. But it also brings a new set of challenges. The risk of the scientific landscape fragmenting into isolated "islands of expertise" is real and threatens to seriously blunt the edge of the new science on drug discovery. The challenge of integration—and specifically of bringing together a diverse pool of scientific talent—has never been greater in the pharmaceutical industry.

Finally, progress in drug science has been cumulative. The older traditional technologies, while yielding center stage to new tools, techniques, and bodies of knowledge, have not gone away, nor are they irrelevant. The story here is not one of new science driving out the old. Medicinal chemistry is still critical to drug discovery in the age of molecular biology. The rDNA technologies first deployed in the mid-1970s are still valid and relevant today; they haven't been replaced by genomics. Indeed, many of the technologies and approaches described in this chapter complement, rather than substitute for, one another. This layering of technological progress again brings with it some interesting and novel organizational challenges. It suggests that organizational learning must also be cumulative. The challenge in this space is not just mastering new technology, but also maintaining capabilities in existing ones.

In essence, these characteristics—the growing size and complexity of the landscape and its intermingling of old and new—create a context that sets the stage for the challenges of the biotechnology business. To gain a fuller appreciation of these challenges, we must turn our attention to the drug R&D process.

3

The Complex Anatomy of Drug R&D

D rugs are deceptively simple products. They have no moving parts. No complicated software. No need for a warranty or maintenance plan. Instructions for use are comparatively straightforward (compared with a typical VCR or other electronic gadget, for example). Surely, development of a new drug cannot be more complicated than development of a new automobile (10,000 parts), an airplane (100,000 parts), or the Windows operating system (about 40 million lines of code). Or can it? In reality, drug R&D is a highly complex process; it is expensive, time consuming, and fraught with risk. In these respects, drug R&D is not too different from, say, the development of a new airliner, a new microprocessor, or even an epic movie.

But drugs *are* different. The potential of drugs to directly affect human well-being is enormous. The latest digital camera may delight you, but it is unlikely to save your life. A buggy piece of software may aggravate you, but it is unlikely to kill you (although it may raise your blood pressure!). Because drugs have the power to save or improve your life *or* the potential to harm you, the stakes are higher than for other kinds of products. This reality pervades many aspects of drug R&D, regulation being the most visible. Drug R&D is different in another, related, way that stems from the complex and highly uncertain nature of human biology. As discussed in the previous chapter, knowledge of human biology has exploded by orders of magnitude in the past decades, and yet many aspects of human biology remain a mystery. As a result, much drug R&D is shrouded in deep uncertainty.

In order to appreciate the revolutionary changes taking place in the drug sciences, as well as understand the fundamental management and economic challenges of companies in the drug business, we need to understand the drug R&D process, and we need to understand its unique characteristics. These characteristics create unique business challenges and explain why strategies and approaches cannot be borrowed wholesale from other contexts.

DRUGS AS COMPONENTS
IN A COMPLEX SYSTEM

Drugs are supposed to change (for the better) the way biological systems inside the body work. In this respect, a drug is akin to a component in a highly complex system. Drug R&D is about finding new components and testing their effect on the system. As discussed in the previous chapter, there are many new technologies for both finding and testing. To understand the kind of problems drug discoverers must overcome, it is useful to illustrate the ways a drug can fail by following the path of a typical drug (in this case, an oral tablet) on its tour through the body.

This pill begins its journey when a patient swallows it, usually with water, milk, or some other liquid. It travels to the gut, where it is broken apart by digestive enzymes. As the pill dissolves, it releases the active ingredient molecules so that they can be absorbed into the bloodstream. But this first step alone is fraught with hazards for the would-be drug. The rate at which the pill dissolves and releases its active ingredient is critical. If the dissolution occurs too slowly, not enough of the active ingredient will be available to the body to have therapeutic effects. If too much of the active ingredient is released too quickly, unwanted side effects might occur. Both the structure and the physical properties of the active ingredient as well as the formulation play a key role in determining how fast dissolution happens.

Once the molecules of active ingredient are free of the pill in which they were delivered, they still face additional hurdles. The digestive enzymes inside the gut may attack the therapeutic agent, alter its structure, and render it useless (this is the reason large biologic molecules like proteins and monoclonal antibodies must be injected; they cannot survive the digestive process in a useful form). The active ingredient—presuming it has survived thus far—must then pass through the walls of the small intestine to be absorbed into the bloodstream. For this to happen, the active ingredient, which enters the body as a dry powder, must be soluble; it must also be absorbed at a particular rate. If absorption is too slow, not enough of the drug may enter the blood stream to have a therapeutic effect. If it is too fast, the possibility of side effects is higher.

Once the active ingredient has made it into the bloodstream, it is transported through the body. The molecule will bind to cell receptors, enzymes, and other targets for which it has an affinity to bind or interact. As discussed in chapter 2, the goal is for the molecule to interact with, or "hit," the targets that prompt the desired therapeutic effect (e.g., block or accelerate production of a certain chemical by the body, up- or down-regulate a certain disease process). The early stages of drug discovery are concerned with identifying the targets that impact a particular disease and finding molecules that hit those particular targets. A drug only works if the right target is chosen and the drug itself hits that target. After it hits the target, it generally triggers a complex cascade of biological reactions that ultimately create the desired therapeutic effect (e.g., lowering blood pressure, stopping cancer cell growth, reducing inflammation).

But even if the drug makes it this far—it gets into the bloodstream and hits the right target for the desired therapeutic effect—its success is still not assured. While the drug may hit the target of interest, it may also bind to other targets with similar structures. In so doing, it may cause another cascade of reactions, and these can lead to other, less desirable, effects. Sometimes these side effects are relatively minor compared with the therapeutic benefits of the drug. But in other cases, side effects can be serious enough to make the drug infeasible as a treatment option. And finally, even if the drug works and its side effects are tolerable (compared with the benefit), the drug has to stay in the body long enough to have its desirable effects but not so long as to trigger undesirable side effects. A drug, like most substances we ingest, does not stay in the body forever (luckily). It is broken down by the body, or *metabolized*. If it is metabolized too quickly, not enough of the drug stays "on board" long enough to deliver its therapeutic benefits. However, if it is metabolized too slowly, it can accumulate, which increases the chance of triggering undesirable side effects. Moreover, drugs that are metabolized in the liver can cause toxic side effects to the liver itself.

This brief (and oversimplified) tour of how drugs work provides some idea of the challenges facing drug R&D. Drugs can fail in many ways. The target could be wrong: it may not play the biological role that it was thought to play. The molecule chosen could be wrong: it may not hit the target of interest, or it may hit the target but also hit other targets, causing deleterious side effects. The molecule may break down too quickly or too slowly in the blood stream. The molecule may be insoluble, or it may break down in the digestive process. The dosage may be incorrect: too much can cause side effects and too little will not have any effect. The formulation has to be designed to enable the drug to be released and absorbed at the right rate. Again, too fast or too slow a rate can be a problem. Finally, the company developing the drug must muster enough data from laboratory studies and human clinical trials to convince regulatory authorities like the FDA to approve the drug for sale.

And these are just the *technical* ways drugs can fail. There are just as many ways drugs can fail commercially and economically. The drug has to be manufacturable. Some drug molecules are so complex that it is very difficult to find feasible manufacturing processes. Or they cannot be manufactured at a cost that will allow the drug to be economically viable. Doctors must be convinced to prescribe the drug, and managed care organizations (and most governments outside the United States) must be convinced to pay for it. Patients must be convinced to take it. And all of these challenges must be tackled amid a rapidly evolving scientific and market landscape.

In many respects, the organizational processes by which drugs are discovered and developed mirrors the path of a drug through the body. While the order of activities varies, each of the potential problems mentioned above is dealt with in a specific phase of the development process. The next section briefly reviews this process.

AN OVERVIEW OF THE DRUG R&D PROCESS

Figure 3-1 provides an illustration of the major phases of work in discovering and developing a drug.[1] Specific tools and technologies mentioned in chapter 2 are referenced in the diagram. To help provide a more concrete illustration of the process, we will use an example of the development of a specific drug and discuss the activities and issues that arise at each stage. The example is hypothetical but draws from the author's observations and analyses of dozens of drug R&D projects over the past decade. The example focuses on a project aimed at finding a new treatment for inflammatory diseases such as rheumatoid arthritis, osteoarthritis, and even some cardiovascular conditions.

Target Identification and Validation

Target identification and validation is concerned with finding the specific biochemical pathway, receptor, protein, or gene that serves as a suitable point for intervention in a disease process. The company in our illustrative example has had a long-term research project aimed at finding drugs for inflammation. A team of molecular biologists, cell biologists, and biochemists, in collaboration with scientists at a university chemical biology department and teaching hospital, was formed to search for a novel target protein involved in inflammation. The team begins with a hypothesis—based on prior scientific research and recent genomic studies—about a specific biochemical pathway that might play a key role in the inflammation. By identifying the pathway—literally the sequence of biochemical reactions that leads to the inflammation—the team hopes to identify a point where a drug might inhibit the process. Molecular geneticists focus on identifying specific genes that might be involved in the disease. Experiments using DNA chips enable the research team to collect data on the expression of thousands of genes that might play a role in the disease. The company's bioinformatics group is asked to cull genetic sequence data from a number of publicly available sources as well as the company's proprietary database to identify potential genes that might be involved.

After slightly more than four years, this process yields a set of potential drug targets. Protein chemists then become involved in

FIGURE 3-1

Phases of the drug R&D process

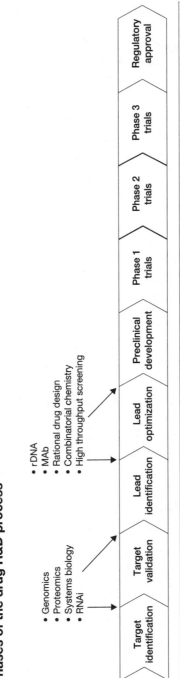

synthesizing and characterizing the potential target proteins. A key issue at this point is which candidate target proteins are "druggable." Not all target proteins are amenable to drug intervention. Researchers need to find a target to which a potential drug molecule will bind. The molecule must also have good pharmaceutical properties—appropriate rates of absorption and metabolism. Structural analysis of the potential binding sites reveals critical problems with some of the targets. For instance, one looks like it could only be "hit" with a molecule that needs to be administered via injection instead of orally. Another target does not have good binding sites, and the company's organic chemists are not optimistic about the prospects of finding a molecule that could hit it. Further analysis reveals that one of the potential protein targets is structurally similar—though not identical—to other proteins that have been successfully targeted by oral drugs. The team now focuses its search on this enzyme.

There are previous studies that provide some evidence that this enzyme is a culprit in inflammation, but there have been no definitive studies. So the team's first task is to validate the target by conducting a series of experiments with "knock-out" mice—mice that have been genetically engineered to both over- and underexpress this particular enzyme. These experiments generate data, but as with most scientific research, the answers are never 100 percent clear-cut: there is a probability distribution. There appears to be a strong statistically significant relationship between the level of inflammation and the level of protein expressed. They do some additional studies that provide additional data consistent with this result. After about six months of experimentation, the team now feels confident that they have a reasonable target for their drug discovery effort. The project is now in its sixth year.

Lead Identification and Optimization

The next step is to find a molecule—a potential drug—that inhibits this enzyme. At this stage, the company's discovery chemistry group becomes involved. Using the structural model of the enzyme, and some prior knowledge, the chemistry group generates some hypotheses about the types of molecules that might inhibit the enzyme.

Several groups are now involved in the project. The computational chemistry group uses computer analysis and modeling to identify molecular structures that are likely to bind to the enzyme. Using both traditional and combinatorial methods, the medicinal chemistry group is synthesizing candidate compounds. And the high throughput screening group is responsible for screening the compounds against the target. Thanks to tools that enable rapid synthesis and screening of molecules, it is possible to test tens of thousands of possible molecules in this phase. At this stage, the researchers are looking for molecules that bind to the target ("hits"); those that do not bind to the target can be eliminated from the search. They further refine their search by limiting screening to molecules that meet certain criteria for "druglike" characteristics.[2]

After this initial "lead identification" process, which takes almost one year of intensive work, they have a number of molecules that look promising. Further work is done to find "analogs" or derivatives of these molecules that might have better properties. This iterative process, known as lead optimization, generates a candidate molecule (CC-25) that looks to have the best fit to the target and is structurally more attractive than the others. It belong to a class of compounds that is not known to cause any particular toxicity problem (but the research team also knows that every molecule is unique and can be full of both pleasant and unpleasant surprises). The team also checks with the company's patent counsel, who confirms that this compound has not been patented by anyone else.

At this stage, the company has a compound that it knows relatively little about. Scientists in the research team know it binds. They do not see anything in the structure that worries them. But, at this stage, they know there is only about a 1-in-5,000 chance that this molecule will work and can be turned into a commercially viable drug. Note, at this stage, that the molecule either *is* or *is not* a "winner." The problem is that the researchers do not know which it is (although given their prior experience, their presumption is that this molecule, like most others, is probably a loser). The task now facing the research team is to conduct a series of in vitro and in vivo experiments to generate data that can tell them whether or not this molecule is worth pursuing in human clinical trials.

Preclinical Development

Preclinical development involves generating data on the safety and potential effectiveness of the candidate compounds prior to testing in humans. This process generally takes about one year. Before the company can test CC-25 in humans, it must evaluate its potential safety and efficacy through an array of both in vitro and in vivo (animal) experiments. The molecule is tested in cell-based assays. Then it will be injected into mice with inflammation. Does it seem to reduce inflammation? Does it cause any toxicities (e.g., liver damage, carcinogenicity)? The research team will also conduct studies in animals to understand the absorption, distribution, metabolism, and excretion rates of the compound (these are known as ADME studies). The results of these experiments provide further data about whether or not this molecule is really the 1-in-5,000 winner. Ultimately, the research team is interested in finding a molecule that will be safe and effective in humans, can be used in a convenient fashion, and can be economically viable. The early stage testing in cell assays and in laboratory animals are models of this process. Mice are biologically different from humans; drugs that work in mice often do not work in people. But animal testing is used to gain clues about the performance of the drug and to identify potential safety issues.

Chances are that our CC-25 molecule will never be tested in humans. It will likely show no effect in laboratory animals or will raise toxicity concerns. Another, "back-up," compound (generally a slight derivation) will then be synthesized and tested. It may take several additional compounds before the experimental data looks promising enough to compile and submit an Investigational New Drug (IND) application and proceed to human testing.

Human Clinical Trials (Phases 1, 2, and 3)

Clinical trials are performed to evaluate the safety and effectiveness of a drug candidate in defined patient populations. These trials are required by the FDA in order to obtain marketing approval. Our would-be drug for inflammation, now called CC-30 (because CC-25, 26, 27, 28, and 29 all failed to meet expectations) is ready for a Phase

1 study in humans. The company has decided to pursue an indication for rheumatoid arthritis, a painful condition affecting joints. The purpose of a Phase 1 study is to assess the drug's safety in a small sample (normally between ten and one hundred) of healthy volunteers. Phase 1 tests of drugs for life-threatening disease (e.g., cancer) can be done in afflicted patients. The Phase 1 trial for CC-30, from the time the first patient was enrolled to the completion of data analysis, required one year and cost the company about $10 million.

If the Phase 1 study demonstrates (at least initially) that CC-30 is safe, the company can proceed to a Phase 2 study. The purpose of a Phase 2 study is to further examine the safety of the drug, as well as the effectiveness of the drug at different doses in the targeted patient population. A typical Phase 2 study involves anywhere from fifty to five hundred patients and may take one to two years to complete. CC-30 is evaluated at five different daily doses (10 mg, 25 mg, 50 mg, 75 mg, and 100 mg). The studies also include a control group of patients who receive only a placebo (this can vary for life-threatening diseases).

The results of the study are promising, but they do not resolve all of the uncertainty. The 10 mg and 25 mg doses showed almost no effect. The 100 mg dose had the best efficacy but also demonstrated a relatively high incidence of potentially troubling side effects (stomach pain and some elevation of liver enzymes). The 50 mg and 75 mg doses had good efficacy and no significant side effects. The medical group prefers the 75 mg dose because it had much stronger efficacy than the 50 mg dose. The process development and manufacturing groups, however, provide an initial estimate of manufacturing costs, and the results trouble the marketing team. CC-30 is a complex molecule that requires fifteen synthetic steps for manufacturing. The costs of producing it will thus be high, and the resulting price for a daily 75 mg treatment would be much higher than a competing product that is likely to gain approval within the next year.

At this stage, senior management asks the project team to pursue two approaches. The process chemistry group is asked to focus on developing a new synthesis that could reduce the cost of manufacturing enough to make a 75 mg tablet economically attractive. Meanwhile, the formulation group is asked to develop alternative formulations that might improve the efficacy of the 50 mg tablet. After a six-month period, both groups have results. The 75 mg tablet can now be made 30 percent less expensively, and some modifications of the formulation appear to enhance the efficacy of the drug. A second set of Phase 2 studies (called Phase 2-B) on both the 50 mg and 75 mg tablets is initiated to confirm the results of work. There is some concern that the 75 mg tablet with the new formulation could exhibit some of the troubling side effects of the original 100 mg tablet, but the data are unclear. However, the 50 mg tablet with the new formulation appears to work exceptionally well and exhibited no serious side effects. Based on these data, a decision is made to go into Phase 3 trials to seek marketing approval for CC-30 (now trade named "Rumotak"). Both the 50 mg and 75 mg doses will be tested. Phase 2 trials for this project cost $40 million and took two years.

The purpose of a Phase 3 study is to confirm the efficacy of the drug in a larger patient group, which usually includes anywhere from hundreds to tens of thousands of patients. Enrolling patients into a study alone is challenging because Phase 3 trials almost always involve multiple clinical trial sites. Patients are typically followed over a longer time period to asses both long-term efficacy and the potential for long-term safety issues. The cost for such trials can be in the range of $50 million to $500 million. Phase 3 studies for Rumotak take almost four years from enrollment to the time to completion of all the studies.

Regulatory Approval

To market a drug, a company must compile all of the drug's results and information into a regulatory marketing application, which it submits to the FDA (or equivalent regulatory body outside the United States) for review. Based on the results of the Rumotak Phase 3 studies, the company submits an application for a new drug approval to the FDA. The data indicate that 60 percent of patients responded exceptionally well to the 50 mg dose, but this was much lower than the 75 percent response rate observed in the Phase 2 studies. The 75 mg dose had about an 85 percent response rate, but some patients experienced stomach discomfort. And a side effect not seen in earlier studies also appears: a slight rash on the arms affected

25 percent of the patients. The rash did not seem to be serious, and so the company seeks approval for both the 50 mg dose and the 75 mg dose. The FDA review process typically takes about one year but can last longer. As is common, the FDA follows up with the company, asking for more clarification on certain Rumotak studies and the interpretation of the results. The FDA approval will determine not only whether the drug can be marketed, but, based on the data, what specific claims the company can make about the drug's performance and profile in their marketing. In the case of Rumotak, the FDA approved the 50 mg dose (1 tablet daily). The 75 mg dose was approved after carefully exploring whether the rash portended any more serious side effects. However, the FDA asked the company to engage in close post-market monitoring of patients on the 75 mg dose to ascertain the longer-term incidence and seriousness of side effects at that dose.

Our illustration of the drug R&D process through the case of CC-25 (later CC-30, and later Rumotak) is very much an exceptional case. As stated before, most drug candidates never make it as far as human testing, and the vast majority of those that do never make it to the market. They are tripped up by safety issues or do not prove to be effective. Even our story of Rumotak may not end with financial success. The sales of the drug may turn out to be much lower than expected; there may be additional competition; there could be regulatory issues or even a patent challenge.

CONCLUSION

This chapter introduced the mechanics of the drug R&D process from start to finish. By now, the reader should have a feel for both the complexity and deep uncertainty of the process. In the next chapter, I delve deeper into the process to understand its salient characteristics and the unique organizational and management challenges it poses.

4

Drug R&D and the Organizational Challenges

R&D is the critical investment in drugs. R&D performance determines competitive performance; the economics of the drug and biotechnology sectors is very much tied to the economics of the R&D. If we want to understand how this business works and what makes it different, we need to understand which characteristics of the R&D process are unique. While drug R&D is similar in many ways to R&D in other sectors, the challenges of drug R&D are dictated, in part, by the limits of biological knowledge and the constraints imposed by human biology. Chapter 3 provided an overview of how the process worked—what happens, when, why. This chapter probes the characteristics of drug R&D that influence the fundamental economics of this business. An analogy to microprocessor design puts drug R&D in a general context and helps focus the discussion in the remainder of the chapter on the unique characteristics and challenges of drug R&D.

IF MICROPROCESSORS WERE LIKE DRUGS

Modern microprocessors—for example, the Intel Dual Core—are mind-bogglingly complex. They can perform billions of calculations

53

per second. They contain millions of circuits packed so tightly that the line widths approach the wavelengths of light. They are manufactured to tolerances that are tighter than almost any other product on earth (a single particle of dust is enough to ruin the whole device). Yet consider that when microprocessor designers start to design a completely new device, they have in front of them clear specifications about what a processor must do (speed, power consumption, etc.). More important, they are given very clear specifications about the system the device will be used in (e.g., a personal computer using a Windows XP operating system). The architecture of the system and the interface between the chip and the systems are clarified up front. Which components and subsystems will interact and which ones function as independent "modules" are specified. And even if the other components have not been specified (e.g., the memory chips, the bus), the designer has general knowledge about what the components will be and what functions they will perform. In the event that some other component of the system is creating a severe constraint, that component itself can be redesigned to accommodate the microprocessor design. Finally, detailed understanding of the system and the physics of chip designs enables designers to use an arsenal of simulation tools to design and test devices in virtual systems before ever etching the design in silicon.

Now consider what the process of chip design might look like if designers worked under the following constraints. They were told to design a chip to solve a very specific problem. They were given some performance specifications (speed, etc.), but they were not given much detail about the computer system the chip would go into. They were not told, for instance, exactly where the chip goes into the system; nor were they given much information on the physical characteristics of the place where the device "plugs in" to the system (e.g., how many pins are needed to plug into the connector). Even worse, they do not have much knowledge about how the chip communicates with the rest of the system. They have only vague knowledge about the other parts of the system that their microprocessor needs to interface with. They can read about much of this in the literature, but they must rely heavily on a reservoir of prior experience with past projects. Moreover, the software that runs the whole system is extraordinarily complex but, alas, not well codified. Our hypothetical designers only get to see fragments of the "source code."

As if this does not already sound like a design nightmare, consider the possibility that the rest of the design of the system this chip will be part of has already been *completely* designed and cannot be changed. Designers cannot ask their colleagues responsible for other components and subsystems to redesign pieces to accommodate their problems. All circuitry has been fixed in place; all the software is done and cannot be altered. The system is what it is. Our hypothetical chip designers must find a design that will fit and function precisely in this complex (and yet not completely understood) system. There are other complications as well. Because of very high interdependencies in the system, small changes in the chip design could have a profound effect on performance (positive or negative). In addition, it turns out that when we manufacture these computers, each one is a little a bit different (but we are not sure how). So our chip might work differently from one machine to the next—or it might not work at all.

If this was the world chip designers worked in, chip design would look very different than it does today. First, most chip development efforts would almost certainly fail. Even those that "worked" would likely work very differently from machine to machine. The design process would largely be one of trial and error, guided by both scientific principles and accumulated experience about what worked (and, more importantly, what did not work) in past projects. The process would also be more complex, in that the chip designer would need to have as much intimate knowledge as possible about other system components. Now, if we think about drugs as components that go into a very complex system (the human body), then the above picture pretty accurately describes the challenges faced by drug R&D scientists.

The microprocessor analogy highlights two salient characteristics of drug R&D that have important implications for the organizational process of drug R&D. First, the process is highly risky due to profound and persistent uncertainty. This uncertainty is rooted in our currently limited knowledge of human biological systems and processes. Second, the nature of the process is integral: it cannot be broken neatly into different pieces. While each of these characteristics surely exists in other sectors, the degree to which both are simultaneously present and exaggerated in drug R&D is unique, with important implications for the economics and management of R&D and the pharmaceutical business as a whole.

PROFOUND AND PERSISTENT UNCERTAINTY

All R&D is by definition uncertain. And uncertainty is by no means unique to drug R&D. However, the nature of the uncertainty is quite distinctive in pharmaceuticals. In most industries, basic technical feasibility is not at stake in the R&D process. Car designers worry a lot about many details of the design and grapple with difficult engineering problems concerning various parts of the vehicle. They likely worry quite a bit about the economic feasibility of the product: Can this design be manufactured? Is this a vehicle that customers will buy? They probably never worry, however, about whether the basic technology is feasible. They can be almost 100 percent certain that at the end of the process they *will* have a vehicle that works. It may end up being a disappointing product, but it will work. The same is true even in relatively high-tech settings like electronics and semiconductors. When Intel engineers set out to develop the next-generation microprocessor, they know with near certainty that they will end up with a device that works. In most contexts fundamental technical uncertainty is resolved fairly early in the process.

In this regard, drug R&D is different. The vast majority of R&D projects fail. The drug candidate under development reveals through testing that it is neither safe nor comparatively effective. Thus when pharmaceutical scientists begin working on a project, they can, in fact, safely assume that after years of effort, they will most likely *not* see their labor bear fruit as a commercially approved drug. In most industries, the term "R&D" is actually a misnomer. Most of the resources and effort go to "development" of already technically feasible concepts.

In pharmaceuticals, the situation is the reverse. Only one in over six thousand compounds synthesized will ever be approved.[1] Historically, even after an Investigational New Drug (IND) application is filed to begin Phase 1 human clinical testing, there is approximately a 60 percent chance that the drug will fail in development before getting to the next phase. A drug that makes it to Phase 2 has only a 50 percent chance of getting to Phase 3. And even when a drug gets to Phase 3 trials, the probability of failure can be as high as 50 percent (depending on the therapeutic category). In other words, if you have a portfolio of ten new drug candidates beginning clinical trials, you would expect that seven would make it to Phase 2, three would make it to Phase 3, and one or two products would ultimately be approved for commercial sale.[2] Consider that the expected probability of success—a project leading to an approved commercial product—does not even reach 50 percent until a drug has completed Phase 2-A clinical studies.[3]

What all this implies is that, in aggregate, the vast majority of resources spent in pharmaceutical R&D goes toward projects that end up being 'losers." Such a relationship is not coincidental. R&D investments in pharmaceuticals are largely focused on testing in order to generate *information* about a drug's potential safety, efficacy, and uses. Posed differently, R&D in pharmaceuticals is fundamentally about successively reducing uncertainty through the acquisition and interpretation of information.

In most contexts, we can think about R&D as involving the evolution of a design. Product development in such industries as automobiles, electronics systems, aircraft, software, and entertainment is a process of imaging and then testing a series of manipulations to the product in order to achieve some desired functional or economic objective. In these contexts, products are not discovered, rather, they evolve through a series of design-test iterations. In an automobile or semiconductor development project, for example, it is meaningful to talk about how a design evolved over time. For example, an initial concept (a high-level depiction of the product) may have been created (designed), and the details of the design were filled in through an iterative process of design and test.

Such a description would not be very accurate with respect to drug R&D. Given our current state of knowledge about drug R&D, it's not meaningful to talk about "designing" drugs the same way we talk about designing electronic circuits. Drug R&D begins with the process of identifying and validating useful therapeutic targets, receptors, hormones, enzymes, and other proteins that might play a role in a disease and that might be a point of intervention for drug therapy. These targets are not designed; they are biological givens. Scientists do not create targets—nature does. Scientists can only find them and figure out what they do and whether they are amenable to some type of drug intervention.

The same is also largely true for the molecules that scientists seek to turn into drugs. Molecules are the products of discovery. "New" molecular entities (organic chemical, biological agents) are in essence not at all new. While molecules can be designed by means of rational drug design techniques, the vast majority already exist (in some form) in nature. They were out there (sometimes in the jungles of South America, sometimes on a shelf in a laboratory) waiting to be found or waiting to find their useful application. Thus drugs do not *evolve* in the same manner as would be true of, say, an automobile or a semiconductor. Such an evolution is not particularly meaningful in the case of drugs. A molecule is initially *selected* for further analysis and testing. If it seems to work, additional tests are performed. This process of testing continues as described in chapter 3. If at any point evidence mounts that this molecule is not a winner, it is abandoned and the process begins again. Posed differently, in the case of drugs, designs are sampled. When they prove problematic, the entire design is abandoned and a new sample is taken (although prior knowledge of failure guides the search for a replacement).

The uncertainty of the search process depends on two factors: prior knowledge that guides identification of potentially attractive options (selection), and good predictive testing models (screening). Both of these are limited in the contexts of many areas of drugs. Despite the extraordinary progress in genetics and molecular biology over the past few decades, it is still extraordinarily difficult for scientists to predict how a particular molecule will work in humans. In many industry contexts today, uncertainty in R&D can be rapidly and efficiently reduced by means of computer simulation models and relatively inexpensive prototype tests (e.g., foam models). But for a model to have predictive accuracy, a deep theoretical understanding of the cause-effect patterns and the interactions among relevant parameters (if X, then Y) is essential. The simulation models used by Boeing's designers are extremely predictive of how a jet will fly because the models are based on fairly precise and well-understood principles of aerodynamics.

Such deep causal knowledge is generally lacking for many areas of biomedical science. It may be understood that a certain protein (when expressed in excess) plays a role in a certain disease, but recent advances in genomics suggest that there are often complex interdependencies among multiple proteins. Inhibiting one may trigger an unexpected cascade of reactions that could have deleterious effects. Weak biological know-how also makes it difficult to extrapolate from the results of animal studies to humans. There have been numerous cancer compounds that have shown dramatic effects in laboratory mice, only to be utterly disappointing in humans. Subtle and not well-characterized differences between mouse biology and human biology are generally responsible for these disappointing results.

Due to the absence of strong prior knowledge and high-fidelity testing models, drug R&D is inherently an iterative and inductive process in which high levels of uncertainty persist throughout the process.

INTEGRALITY

Virtually all R&D involves solving many types of problems. Moreover, the solutions to all these problems must be compatible, if not integrated, to work as a whole. The challenge of integration is easy to see with highly complex physical systems, such as microprocessors, electronics equipment, automobiles, and airplanes. In these contexts, the parts (including software) must literally fit and function together, and the results of poor integration quickly become apparent in the appearance and performance of the system. As discussed earlier, drugs are not physically complex products with many moving and functionally interdependent parts. Nevertheless, their development requires a high degree of integrated problem solving across different scientific, technical, and functional domains.

While all products, to some degree, require integration, the approach to integration varies greatly across contexts. In some cases, a big problem can be broken down into a set of relatively independent subproblems. The ability to break a problem up in this way is known as *modularity*. With modular design solutions, each subproblem (or module) contains a relatively independent set of tasks and problem-solving activities. A desktop computer is a good example of a highly modular system. The critical subsystems and components—microprocessor, memory, hard disk, graphics card, sound board, software, keyboard, monitor, and so forth—must all be able to work together. However, because of well-defined interfaces between the components and standards for how these subsystems should relate to one another, they can each be designed somewhat independently. There is a high degree of interdependence within modules (e.g., the microprocessor) but a high degree of independence across modules.[4] Modularity generally requires well-defined interfaces and standards specifying how different components of the system are supposed to fit and function together. For instance, consider a typical Windows-based personal computer. The Windows operating system and Intel X86 microprocessor provide a set of standards, or architecture, that specifies how the other components should fit and function together. As a result, various components (software applications, graphics cards, storage, etc.) can be developed relatively independently of one another.

There are many advantages to modularity.[5] For instance, because it enables parallel development of subsystems, modularity facilitates strategies for reducing development lead times. It also expands opportunities for experimentation and improvement, thus potentially leading to more rapid rates of innovation. Modularity can also have a profound effect on industry structure, and organizational boundaries in particular. Because it reduces the complexity and costs of coordinating development across subsystems, modularity generally facilitates outsourcing of those subsystems.[6] Again, the PC industry is a good example. The modularization of the PC architecture paved the way for the widespread outsourcing of components and subsystems to outside suppliers. Competition among suppliers of any given module (e.g., the hard drive) can stimulate innovation and also lead to lower costs.

At the other end of the spectrum are integral systems or integral problems. In contrast to modularity, integrality implies a high degree of interdependence or interconnectedness among components or problems. With integral systems, the solution to one problem either shapes or is shaped by solutions to other problems. Problem solving in these contexts requires a kind of joint optimization across different problem domains. The body of a car is a highly integral design. Any given look (e.g., sporty) is the result of how a broad constellation of design elements and design cues come together in subtle ways. For instance, a decision about how the front hood should slope cannot be made without taking into consideration the angle of the front windshield pillars, the geometry of the side panels, and so forth. This is why car companies generally assign a single team to the body styling.

Drugs are an example of an integral product. This may seem surprising in light of the fact that there are very few components to partition. The vast majority of drugs consist of an active chemical or biological ingredient and the inactive ingredients needed for formulation. It is tempting to think of these as the two basic "modules" of the drug, but that would not be quite accurate. The active ingredient and the formulation are not independent; the design of the formulation depends on the properties of the active molecule. While there are standard approaches to formulation, there is usually a high degree of customization between the formulation and the molecule. Ultimately, the performance of the drug (safety, efficacy) is jointly determined by the active molecule and the formulation. The pharmacological performance of a molecule with, say, poor absorption properties might be improved substantially through the design of the formulation (and vice versa).

Yet the problem is even more complex than this. Go back to the concept of a drug as a component that is put into a system (the human body). Human biology is a highly complex, highly integral system. And human biology is a given. It is not in the power of the drug research scientist to make that system modular. There are places where biology is modular, and there are places where it is not. It is not always known which systems fall into which categories. The integral nature of biological systems makes it difficult to partition, or modularize, the underlying problem-solving processes. Even if the physical characteristics of a drug do not lend themselves easily to modularization, is it possible to think about the various functional and technical activities (e.g., target discovery and validation, lead identification and optimization, toxicology, process development, clinical trial design) required for drug R&D as independent "modules"? While it is possible to break apart certain activities, the various elements of drug R&D—from discovery through regulatory approval—tend to be highly interdependent.

Consider the problem of identifying a target for drug discovery. The big questions to be resolved are, What is the underlying mechanism of the disease, and where might drug therapy intervene in this process? Because human biology is extraordinarily complex, target identification is a multifaceted problem, with many interdependent issues. What is the pathway? What genes might be at work? How do they interact? What are the proteins these genes express, and what do they do? What is the structure of those proteins? How likely is one or more of these proteins to be a "druggable" target? Answering these questions requires insights from different disciplines (e.g., structural genomics, functional genomics, cell biology, molecular biology, protein chemistry) and a broad range of approaches (computational methods, high throughput experimentation, traditional "wet" biology, etc.).

The same type of integration must also occur further downstream in development but with different disciplines, such as toxicology, process development, formulation design, clinical research, biostatistics, regulatory affairs, and marketing. It is hard, if not downright impossible, to successfully develop a drug by solving one problem at a time in isolation because each technical choice (the target you pursue, the molecule you develop, the formulation, the design of the clinical trial, the choice of the target patient population, the choice of manufacturing process, etc.) has implications for other technical choices. Here again, an example may be helpful.

Consider a drug candidate for cancer in early-stage human clinical trials. It is a novel compound that targets a receptor on the surface of the cancer cells. This receptor is hypothesized to play a critical role in the cascade of biochemical reactions that lead to uncontrolled cell growth. However, despite the fact that the active ingredient significantly reduced tumor size in laboratory animals, the early results in human trials are disappointing. A small percentage of patients seem to respond well; they get a very significant reduction in tumor size that appears to be durable. Another group of patients gets a temporary reprieve. But, unfortunately, many patients seem to get no benefit. What's going on?

There are many possible explanations for such a result, but the information required to solve the puzzle is likely to come from various sources. One possibility is that the receptor actually does not play the role previously hypothesized. Maybe interfering with this receptor has no impact at all on cancer growth. Maybe the effect of this receptor on cancer depends on what is happening simultaneously with several other receptors. Perhaps this receptor plays an important role in cancer cells that grow in lab animals, but not in humans. Another possibility is that the target receptor is part of a family of closely related receptors: interfering with one subtype has a powerful effect, while interfering with the others has little effect. Perhaps the structure of the target receptor varies slightly across different people due to genetics (the responders may have the subtype targeted by the drug molecule). Of course, cancer cells themselves are highly prone to mutation, and perhaps the target receptor itself actually changes over time in some patients. This could help to explain why the drug worked well for some time in some patients but not in others.

Of course, maybe the target receptor is actually the correct one, but the molecule being tested is not the right one. Perhaps the candidate molecule does not bind well to the target. There could be subtle differences in the molecule initially tested in early research and the one being tested on humans. Or perhaps the structure molecule is somehow being altered in the body as it is absorbed and metabolized. This could call for changes in the formulation. Maybe different patients metabolize the same drug differently: for some patients it is absorbed and metabolized in a way that keeps the molecule potent, but for others it is getting degraded. It could also be the case that the doses are not correct. We might see a stronger, more curable effect in a greater number of patients if we tried the drug at a higher dose. Of course this could raise issues of side effects and toxicity that would need to be checked. Perhaps the drug would work better if we administered it to patients whose cancers were in earlier stages of development. Maybe a different clinical trial design (e.g., more patients, testing the drug in combination with another anticancer agent) would provide stronger results.

If this seems like the proverbial Gordian knot, it is. There is no way to sort out what is happening by just looking at one aspect of the problem or by looking at each aspect of the problem in isolation. While exploring the plausibility of these various explanations requires the expertise of different kinds of scientists, very dense information flows would be required among them to arrive at a solution. It is also clear that the problem-solving process is iterative across these domains. We can think of the various technical and functional domains involved as shining a light on one aspect of the problem. To discover and successfully develop a drug, one needs to illuminate the whole problem. One beam of light is generally not enough.

DRUG R&D IN THE "AGE OF BIOTECHNOLOGY"

Popular accounts of biotechnology and academic writings on the topic posit that advances in biomedical science will transform the process of drug R&D. While this is, by and large, true, it is often assumed that the science will dramatically reduce the organizational challenges of R&D by both dramatically reducing uncertainty and by simplifying the process. A closer reflection on the science, however, should give us pause. Below, I argue that in fact the advances in the science are, at least at this stage, likely to increase the uncertainty and increase the organizational complexity of the process.

The Impact of the New Science on Uncertainty

Chapter 2 recounted an extremely fast and broad expansion in the size of the scientific landscape. What effect has this expanding scientific frontier had on the uncertainty of drug discovery? Before attempting to answer this specific question, we must consider the usual relationship between science and R&D uncertainty. Prior research on the impact of scientific knowledge on technical problem solving posits that science reduces the uncertainty in R&D by providing causal theories and "first principles." Such theories and principles, which highlight feasible solutions to a problem and provide guidance about the characteristics of good solutions, are supposed to reduce the randomness of the search process.[7] Much of the literature on the impact of scientific know-how on R&D has focused on how scientific knowledge enhances searches by illuminating attractive options.[8] As a result, a scientific advance is supposed to make R&D more efficient by essentially narrowing down the options that scientists might consider. The semiconductor is a good example of an invention that fundamentally altered the feasible options for electronic system design. Knowledge about aerodynamics provides guidance about the kind of wing design an aeronautical engineer might investigate to find one that is feasible.

It is often assumed that the new science of biotechnology would have a similar effect on drug R&D. That is, it would provide a set of first principles that enabled a more rational (i.e., less random, less *uncertain*) drug discovery process. Indeed, one of the assumptions often made by investors (and entrepreneurs) in biotechnology is that the science would transform the economics of drug R&D by dramatically reducing attrition rates of drug candidates (the single biggest cost driver of drug R&D).

Scientific advances, as noted above, have opened up new frontiers. But these advances have not necessarily reduced uncertainty in R&D. If anything, the initial expectations more often than not proved to be wrong, or at least needed to be modified. Consider the following examples. When rDNA first came onto the scene in the late 1970s, there were very high expectations for recombinant proteins as drugs. At the very least, they were supposed to be safer than chemically synthesized drugs because they were "natural." They were also viewed as potentially more effective because they harnessed molecules from the body's own disease-fighting machinery. The rise of biotechnology-based drugs was supposed to signal the end of chemical drugs. Human clinical testing of rDNA products showed these to be flawed assumptions. rDNA-derived proteins, just like chemically synthesized drugs, could also have nasty side effects. And once outside the domain of well-understood and well-known "replacement" proteins (e.g., insulin, human growth hormone, Factor VIII), the success rate of rDNA proteins has proved to be no higher than that of chemically synthesized drugs.[9]

A similar pattern played out in monoclonal antibodies (MAbs). Initially viewed as "magic bullets" because of their ability to bind to specific disease targets, first-generation MAbs derived from mouse cells generally failed because they caused an immune response in humans. Not until scientists at Genentech figured out how to "humanize" MAbs did this technology begin to demonstrate success in the clinic. Combinatorial chemistry was supposed to make traditional ("manual") methods of medicinal chemistry obsolete. Initial applications of combinatorial chemistry proved to be disappointing, as many of the compounds produced were not biologically active. It turned out that medicinal chemists' knowledge of the structural characteristics that make compounds biologically active is critical to the search for drugs.

Genomics is another fascinating example of how advances in the science often help us understand more about what we do *not* know than what we know. It was formerly believed that the human genome contained somewhere between 80,000 and 125,000 genes. Only once the Human Genome Project was completed did it become surprisingly apparent that the true figure probably lay in the neighborhood of 25,000 to 30,000.[10] And without functional knowledge about what each gene does, it is difficult to use this knowledge to advance the search for drugs.

The above examples suggest that with advances in the science, the level of uncertainty in the technological environment may have actually increased rather than decreased. How did this happen? There are four basic characteristics of the scientific landscape that exacerbate the uncertainty of drug discovery processes.

First, a large range of options (more targets, more potential compounds, more approaches) means more uncertainty. This may sound counterintuitive at first, but it is not. Consider the following example. You're hiking in the mountains and there is only one feasible path to take. It may not be a very good path. It might be dangerous. You are not even sure it will get you home. But you have no choice since it is the only path. In terms of your course of action, there is no uncertainty. Your outcome may be uncertain, but your action is not. If you have a thousand possible paths, you have to make choices, and there is uncertainty associated with the outcome of each choice. The same holds true in drug discovery. Scientists have a much bigger array of choices to explore in trying to find a treatment for a disease. They have more options, but they have more chances to get it wrong as well. There are more blind alleys.

The problem of more choice would not necessarily lead to more uncertainty if we had better information about the likely outcomes of those choices. If you have a good map, with all the trails well marked, then the extra choices are not a problem. You can eliminate from consideration the trails that will not get you home. Even if the map is imperfect, it is still a start: it allows you to deal with uncertainty by eliminating certain options from consideration and focusing your trial-and-error on the most promising paths. Earlier, I noted that science is sometimes likened to a map; it points the way.[11] But this characterization assumes the science has matured. It assumes that the terrain being explored has been mapped before (by another pioneer). In biotechnology, we are still in the field's infancy, despite massive progress in the past three decades. In drugs, there is a much broader array of options to explore, but very little is actually known about the feasibility of these options. Historically, when drug discovery was limited to the neighborhood of small molecules and about five hundred targets, a great deal was known about the neighborhood. There were not many targets, but they were well understood. Scientists used to spend entire careers studying a specific drug target or class of targets. With the recent explosion in number of targets, we just have not had the chance to really understand each target in depth. To use the old aphorism, our knowledge is a mile wide but an inch deep. Thus as we venture out onto the vast frontier, we find that we do not have very good maps and must engage in more, not less, trial and error.

The cumulative nature of scientific progress would suggest that over time, uncertainty will recede. And this is very likely. However, one of the challenges in drugs is the long lag times between discovery of a concept and the proof of its feasibility. One of the interesting, and perhaps unique, challenges of the drug sciences revolution is that it is characterized by a combination of rapid cadence of scientific advance and long lag times for validation. Few would question that the sheer pace of scientific advance in this space over the past thirty years has been extraordinary. Every few years, a new technological trajectory has sprouted from the fruits of scientific research: rDNA, MAbs, structure-based drug design, high throughput screening, genomics, proteomics, systems biology, and, most recently, RNA interference. At the same time, to fully understand and validate the applicability of any new technology for drug discovery requires many years of further development and testing. The "next" wave has usually arrived before the "old" wave of technology was optimally utilized or even understood.

As a result, much of the landscape is actually quite poorly mapped. Consider the following example. Genomics and other basic biological research have identified tens of thousands of potential new targets for drug discovery. But it takes an enormous amount of time and effort to fully validate these targets. As noted earlier, many scientists involved in drug research maintain that a target can only be considered validated if there is extensive evidence from human clinical trials that a specific drug has beneficial therapeutic effects by hitting that target. Our ability to identify new targets has outpaced our ability to study them and validate their biological roles. A report released in 2001 by Lehman Brothers, with the support of McKinsey & Company, presented the findings of a survey of forty pharmaceutical company executives. Results show that thirteen years ago, a researcher studying a particular drug target could consult an average of more than a hundred literature references. By 2002, with the explosion in potential targets, the figure had declined to an average of eight publications per target.[12]

On one level, our knowledge has expanded. We conduct the drug discovery game over a much larger landscape, thanks to the genomics and the explosion of new drug targets. Our map is indeed larger. But as we get closer to the "frontier," the detail of our map is, not surprisingly, much poorer than in the neighborhoods we have roamed for years.

Effects of the New Science on Integrality

It was argued above that the drug discovery game is played on a much bigger landscape than it was before the advent of the biotech industry. But the landscape is not just bigger, it is also, thanks to the developments discussed in chapter 2, much more diverse. Drug researchers today are armed with a much broader array of tools in the search for new drugs. To find biologically relevant targets, for instance, they can draw from genomics, proteomics, system biology, computational genomics, antisense, RNA interference, gene chip technology, as well as deepening reservoirs of biomedical research (e.g., immunology, cancer biology). To find molecules that might work on these targets, they can use traditional medicinal chemistry, combinatorial chemistry, chemical biology, rDNA, MAbs, biophysics, computational chemistry, and high throughput screening. This expansion in the breadth of the drug discovery tool kit is unambiguously a good thing. Diseases such as cancer are tricky adversaries, and these different tools shed light on different parts of a complex puzzle. However, as discussed in chapter 3, in order to exploit the potential of these tools, they need to be used in concert; that is, they need to be integrated.

The need for integration in drug discovery is not unique. In any given context, R&D typically draws from many distinct bodies of knowledge. For instance, car body design must mesh knowledge about materials, mechanical engineering, aerodynamics, acoustics, and aesthetics. Microprocessors embody technical choices about materials, software algorithms, circuit designs, packaging, and lithographic processes. Integration across technologies and technical disciplines is in fact *the* essential challenge of product development.[13]

Integration is facilitated when there is a dominant logic or architecture about how the various "pieces of the puzzle" are supposed to fit together. Kuhn used the term *scientific paradigm* to describe a commonly accepted set of theories, assumptions, models, principles, and methods that provide intellectual coherence to fields of science.[14] Paradigms define which problems are important (relevant) and which approaches are acceptable for solving those problems. Building on this notion, Giovanni Dosi introduced the idea of *technological paradigms* as a shared "outlook" (held by engineers and scientists) about the most relevant technical problems and the accepted tools, methods, and principles for addressing those.[15] Scientific paradigms are generally grounded in bodies of theory (e.g., Newtonian physics); technological paradigms are very often manifested in specific physical designs that become a reference point for future design changes (e.g., the DC-3 aircraft, the IBM-360 computer, the Intel X86 microprocessor).

The emergence of a paradigm in scientific fields and in technological domains is important for three reasons. First, because the paradigm provides a shared set of accepted theories, principles, methods, and approaches, it facilitates cumulative progress. Work conducted by different people and different organizations can be connected over time in a cumulative manner. For example, once the IBM-360 had become established, it defined an agenda for a stream of future developments in computer systems, subsystems, and peripherals. Second, by providing a conceptual architecture for different technologies and bodies of knowledge, the paradigm itself becomes a mechanism for integration. This was essentially the role played by medicinal chemistry in drug R&D during much of the postwar era.

Finally, the emergence of new paradigms has the potential to affect competition and industry structure. Historians of science and technology focus on the processes by which new theories, paradigms, and bodies of technology compete with and ultimately replace existing ones. The notion that new approaches disrupt old ones is firmly embedded in the literature on technological change and has greatly influenced how both scholars and practitioners think about the challenge of innovation. For instance, one of the empirical patterns found in many previous studies of technical progress is that new technologies threaten the economic viability of established firms by making their technical competences obsolete.[16]

The impact of scientific advance in drug research appears to be more complex. There is not yet a dominant paradigm for drug discovery. The biotechnology revolution ushered in many new tools and approaches, but it did not augur a new paradigm of drug discovery that drove out the old. While there are clearly instances where new tools and techniques for drug discovery do drive out existing approaches—for example, automation drove out manual methods for gene sequencing and humanized monoclonal antibodies have replaced murine antibodies—parts of the landscape discovered years ago are by no means obsolete. Traditional medicinal chemistry still plays a key role in drug discovery. It complements and is complemented by new methods such combinatorial chemistry, molecular modeling, and high throughput screening. Chemical compounds discovered fifty years ago continue to be screened today against newly discovered targets. Likewise, targets identified thirty years ago are still the focus today of drug discovery efforts.

As described earlier, the history of the drug sciences revolution is very much one of successive "waves" of new technology that rise up and later become adapted into the flow. Recombinant DNA and MAbs represented the first waves of biotechnology that came on the scene in the late 1970s. Many predicted that new methods of making drugs based on genetic engineering would replace traditional "old" medicinal chemistry. This has not happened; moreover, it now turns out that medicinal chemistry and genetic engineering are complementary. This pattern has repeated itself over the subsequent thirty years, with the emergence of rational drug design, combinatorial chemistry, and high throughput screening; then genomics, proteomics, and more recently, systems biology and RNA interference. Each new approach emerges from science and initial expectations (and hype) are that this one is "the real deal" and will dominate. But there has been little replacement of old with new. Instead, the new technologies, as well as the even newer ones, coexist with the old. Furthermore, it appears that they do not operate independently; rather, they are often highly complementary.

While each new wave has opened up new areas for exploration, no approach was made obsolete by the next. As a result of this process of technological accumulation, the drug sciences landscape has thus become highly heterogeneous, with distinct bodies of knowledge and multiple scientific disciplines coexisting. As stated in the first chapter, this is the essential challenge of describing and naming the scientific revolution in drugs over the past thirty years. It is not biotechnology; it is not genomics or proteomics; it is not rational drug design; it is not computational chemistry; it is not high throughput screening. Rather, the field of drug sciences—biotechnology—is all of these: it encompasses a broad constellation of technologies, methodologies, and disciplines.

While adding new tools to the kit has clear potential benefits, it also creates organizational challenges. The complementary nature of the tools suggests that an approach that integrates approaches would be highly fruitful. Yet integration is made difficult by the fact that these diverse approaches originate from different disciplines, each

with its own logic and languages. And people trained in these different disciplines often attack similar problems very differently. Indeed,
each approach may define a different primary problem and embed
distinctive biases about what constitutes a fruitful approach.

Consider some of the different research strategies used in the
search for more effective cancer treatments. An rDNA approach to
drug discovery restricts the search for new drugs to that part of the
landscape occupied by proteins found in the human body. In this
approach, the search for a new drug begins with identification of a
protein that—through absence or malformation—causes a particular
disease. In the case of cancer, this might mean trying to find those
proteins that stimulate the immune system's ability to respond.
Because rDNA is a means of producing protein molecules, the
approach always begins with the question: What protein can we add
to potentially ameliorate or cure the disease?

A second approach is to stimulate the body's immune system via
a therapeutic vaccine. There have been a number of attempts over
the past two decades to develop cancer vaccines that do this. The
strategy involves identifying the unique characteristics of cancer cells
that can be incorporated into a vaccine, and thus fool the body into
mounting a strong immunologic reaction. The focus of this strategy is
very much on identifying what cancer cells (and in particular the surface of such cells) look like to the immune system. This approach can
utilize rDNA techniques since many of the distinguishing features of
cancer cells are receptors, which are themselves proteins. Like the
rDNA approach, the vaccine strategy is deeply rooted in immunology
and cell biology.

Gene therapy provides yet another approach. It begins with an
assumption that specific genes are responsible for the rapid growth
and immortality of cancer cells. Rather than trying to harness the
body's immune system (as is the case for rDNA and vaccines), gene
therapy seeks to directly alter the "problem" genes of the cancer cells
themselves. In essence, it tries to turn cancer cells into normal cells.
This approach is clearly rooted in genetics and specifically cancer
genetics. It requires finding out what genes are responsible for the
properties of a cell that make it cancerous.

Monoclonal antibodies offer yet another approach to cancer therapy. As with vaccines, this approach often begins by trying to charac-

terize the unique structural features of the cancer cell surface (e.g., what receptors are found on the surface of the cancer cell). Once such receptor sites are found, the strategy is to engineer an antibody that can bind selectively to a specific site on the surface of the cancer cell. And even here, there are two possible strategies. One is to conjugate or attach to the antibody some toxic agent that can kill the cancer cell. Thus the antibody is a vehicle to selectively deliver a toxic agent that would kill the cancer cell while leaving healthy cells untouched. Another approach is to use the antibody to "gum up" the receptors directly involved in uncontrolled cell growth. This is how a drug like Herceptin works against certain kinds of breast cancers. Researchers discovered that a specific receptor (EGF) can be found on certain breast cancers. By blocking this receptor (via an antibody), the cell is not able to receive growth signals.

A small-molecule approach considers yet other angles on the problem. One of the biggest advances in cancer research has involved gaining a deeper understanding of the chain of biochemical reactions responsible for cancerous cell growth. The drug research strategy for this approach is to find a molecule that can inhibit or block one of the key reactions in the chain. An example would be Aurora kinases, a family of enzymes that appear to play an important role in the growth and proliferation of cancer cells. Research has shown that Aurora kinases are overexpressed in a number of types of cancer cells. Armed with this knowledge, researchers following this strategy look for (by means of high throughput screening and combinatorial chemistry) or design (by means of rational drug design) a molecule that inhibits these kinases.

Each one of the above approaches is currently being used and explored for cancer drug R&D. Each has a very specific bias about what the most important problem is and what is likely to be a good or bad approach. While they are all related in trying to solve the same problem, they come at the problem in very different ways. They draw from distinct bodies of knowledge. They focus on different aspects of the problems. They involve distinctive sets of downstream challenges such as clinical trial design, regulatory strategy, manufacturing, and distribution.

Discussions with researchers who work with each of these approaches are often quite fascinating. They describe their own approaches with great enthusiasm and elegance and are often quick to point out the "fatal flaw" of other approaches. In essence, these approaches have come to generate distinct bodies of knowledge. Ironically, while they draw on some similar scientific bases, research communities often operate as separate islands of expertise. Each approach is rooted in well-established bodies of science, but emotional attachment to one's own favored approach can be strong. This is natural and, indeed, somewhat healthy. The scientific landscape has produced many different potential approaches, and the high degree of parallel experimentation likely increases the chances of finding good solutions. Yet while these approaches are distinctive, they are potentially complementary. Knowledge gleaned about cancer-specific receptors is likely to be valuable to researchers following any of the above approaches.

Thus one of the great benefits of the biotechnology revolution is that it has broadened the landscape. It has not only opened many new frontiers, but it has opened many different frontiers in the form of new approaches, tools, and research strategies. Yet at that same time, this diversity in the environment has also increased the challenges of integration. We have more distinct specialists, not fewer. We have more disciplinary languages, not fewer. And recall that amidst all the new stuff, we still have plenty of "old" technology and approaches that are highly relevant. The breadth of capability, skill, and knowledge needed to operate effectively in this drug landscape has increased, not decreased. Yet the need for integration has become even more important.

CONCLUSION: TOWARD A SET OF "DESIGN SPECS" FOR THE BIOTECHNOLOGY SECTOR

This chapter completes part I of this book. The science and the R&D process represent a critical aspect of the landscape in which the biotechnology sector operates. It is not, however, the only one; regulatory and political issues, social forces, and market and economic forces also serve to constrain and shape this sector. If one wants to understand the business of biotech and the challenges of operating in this sector, the characteristics of the science and the R&D process must be understood. The goal of part I has been to identify the features of the scientific landscape and R&D process that shape the challenges of businesses operating in this environment.

Part II will turn to the business implications of these features. As a preface to those chapters, it is useful to ask the following hypothetical question: If you could design this sector from scratch, what specific problems would you design it to solve? In essence, these problems define the "functional specifications" of the business. What would we need it to do well? Three themes emerge from the discussion of the science and R&D in the previous chapters: risk, integration, and learning.

Risk

There is little doubt that this is a highly risky sector. Most development efforts fail in the face of profound and persistent uncertainty. While the science is progressing, it is not necessarily leading to the short-term reduction in technical uncertainty that many had hoped for. Thus, to function as a business, the biotechnology sector needs appropriate mechanisms for efficiently managing risks and encouraging and rewarding risk taking. These mechanisms fall into various categories. Risk is driven by uncertainty, and uncertainty is essentially a lack of information. Thus mechanisms to generate and disseminate relevant information play a critical role in the efficient management of risk. Another critical element of risk management is the arrangements for funding risky investments and for rewarding those who bear those risks. Thus we need to explore how the biotechnology sector gets funded and the mechanisms for appropriating returns on those investments.

Integration

The scientific revolutions of the past thirty years have added many new weapons to the arsenal of drug discovery and development. But these tools, like pieces of a jigsaw puzzle, are really only effective when used in combinations. As the scientific knowledge base of drug

R&D broadens, the challenges of integrating the relevant pieces become even more difficult and important. To perform well, the sector requires appropriate mechanisms for bringing together and integrating the right mix of cross-disciplinary talents, skills, and capabilities. These mechanisms include organizational structures and strategies and the means by which different types of organizations (large firms, small start-ups, universities, etc.) interact. However, the sector also requires micro-organizational mechanisms for creating truly integrated problem solving and avoiding islands of specialization. And, perhaps most importantly, it requires ways of getting together the right mix of people from different scientific and functional backgrounds to collaborate and exchange information.

Learning

Given both deep uncertainty and high complexity, it should not be surprising that "failure" is routine in drug R&D. Yet we need to be careful of the word failure: in this context perhaps more than in any other, every project is truly an experiment. As such, every project—whether it results in an approved drug or yet another shelved effort—generates valuable information and lessons about future paths. Because failure is so common, learning from the failures—both technical lessons and organizational lessons—is essential to improve productivity and performance over time. Thus this sector needs mechanisms for capturing and leveraging learning from experience.

The next chapters will examine how well the biotech sector achieves these objectives, exploring the organizational structures and forms, institutional arrangements, strategies, management practices, and other forces that shape how the biotechnology sector works. Throughout these chapters, we must keep in mind the question, Is this sector structured to facilitate the requisite risk management, integration, and learning?

PART II

THE BUSINESS OF THE SCIENCE

5

The Anatomy of a
Science-Based Business

The focus in earlier chapters was on the *science of the business*, and the particular requirements imposed by the science on the business. This section turns to the *business of the science*. Are those requirements fulfilled?

This chapter begins to explore the anatomy of the business, examining such questions as: What types of firms compete in this segment? How have these changed over time? What kind of strategies have they pursued? and, What capabilities do they have? In addressing these questions, the chapter explores three major themes.

- First, it describes the emergence of biotechnology as a new segment of the pharmaceutical industry.

- Second, it analyzes how firm capabilities have evolved over time.

- Finally, it presents the role of established pharmaceutical companies and the emergence and evolution of the market for know-how.

Like living entities, industries are not designed, but they do have designs. In the case of living systems, we generally refer to the design as the *anatomy*, which characterizes the parts and how they relate to one another. Anatomy is important for understanding the performance of living things. Evolutionary biological theory teaches us that anatomies of species evolve over time in response to environmental pressures. Industries also have anatomies, and these anatomies evolve over time in response to environmental pressures such as changes in science, technology, and customers' needs.

Metaphorically speaking, determining the fit between the science and the business is akin to determining the relationship between a geographic landscape and the anatomy of the species that live there. If you know about the geography of a place (e.g., climate or terrain), you can begin to understand the kinds of species that thrive in that environment. For instance, the coats of seals help them thrive in arctic climates but would doom them in the tropics. In our context, the science is a key piece of the landscape. It defines what is known and what is not; what the relevant problems are, and how they should be pursued. The science determines the context and creates specific organizational and economic challenges.

The anatomy of an industry encompasses: (1) the direct *participants* in the industry (start-up firms, established companies, universities, not-for-profit laboratories, investors, customers, etc.); (2) *institutional arrangements* that connect these players (capital markets, market for know-how, product markets, the grant allocation process); and (3) the *rules* that govern and influence how these institutional arrangements work. Figure 5-1 provides an overview of the anatomy of the biotechnology sector as described in this book: the participants are shown in boxes; the institutional arrangements—the metaphorical "connective tissue"—are shown as lines; and the rules are shown in circles. This diagram belies the enormous complexity underlying this industry. It is by no means comprehensive; rather, it illustrates at a fairly high level of abstraction the major types of players, connections, and rules that drive the business.

The present investigation will not probe all corners of the diagram—such a task is beyond the scope of this book. Rather, since the subject at hand is the interaction of science and business, I will focus most heavily on those parts of the anatomy that connect businesses to science, specifically, three sets of players (and the interactions among them) that have directly participated in the development and application of the science: universities, new biotech firms, and estab-

FIGURE 5-1

The anatomy of the biotechnology business

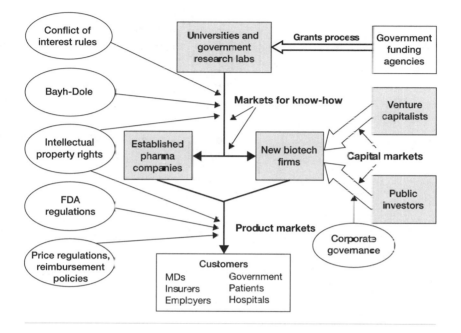

lished pharmaceutical companies. Consideration will also be given to the influence of investors (venture capitalists and public equity investors) and the capital markets on the behaviors and strategies of companies in the sector. This chapter is primarily historical, tracing the evolution of the biotechnology sector over a number of waves of entry, each of which was associated with specific technological strategies and business models.

EMERGENCE OF THE "BIOTECHNOLOGY" SEGMENT OF THE PHARMACEUTICAL INDUSTRY

The year 1976 marks a watershed in the evolution of the pharmaceutical industry. Prior to that year, there had been no successful entry into the pharmaceutical industry since the founding of Syntex (a pioneer in the development of birth control pills) in 1944. High fixed costs and risks of development were a major barrier to entry. The technology of drug R&D—random screening—itself acted as a barrier to entry. The vast "chemical libraries" built by existing pharmaceutical companies over decades of R&D gave them a competitive advantage in the era of random screening.

The erosion of major entry barriers began in 1976, when Genentech, the first specialized "biotechnology" firm, was founded. As mentioned in chapter 2, in 1973, Herbert Boyer and Stanley Cohen invented a technique for genetically engineering the DNA of cells (recombinant DNA, or rDNA, technology). A young venture capitalist named Robert Swanson, upon reading about the scientists' discovery, called Boyer and requested a meeting. Boyer agreed to give Swanson ten minutes of his time. The meeting, held in January 1976, lasted for three hours, and at its conclusion the two agreed to form a company.[1] Genentech was formally incorporated in April of that year.

Since that time, the biotechnology sector has witnessed the entry of hundreds of newly formed biotechnology firms. Figure 5-2 shows the patterns of entry of new firms by year and by core technology.[2] A few observations can be made from these data. First, while entry has occurred over much of the sector's history, the pattern of entry has been highly cyclical. There appear to be three distinct generations of entry: 1976–1985, 1986–1992, and 1992–2000. The apparent decline in entry after 2000 may simply reflect that later entrants into the industry are still disproportionately privately held firms and thus do not appear in the sample.

Second, as discussed in chapter 2, the technological landscape is highly variegated and heterogeneous. There is no single "biotechnology" but instead many technologies. This complexity is reflected in the new firms that enter the industry. From a technological point of view, the biotechnology sector is composed of subsegments with distinct technological approaches and strategies. Indeed, the depiction in figure 5-2 probably obscures some of the underlying technological diversity. In order to avoid making the picture excessively complex, related technologies are consolidated. For instance, the "genomics" category includes not only classical genomics companies like Celera

FIGURE 5-2

Waves of entry of biotechnology firms by core technology

Number of
companies

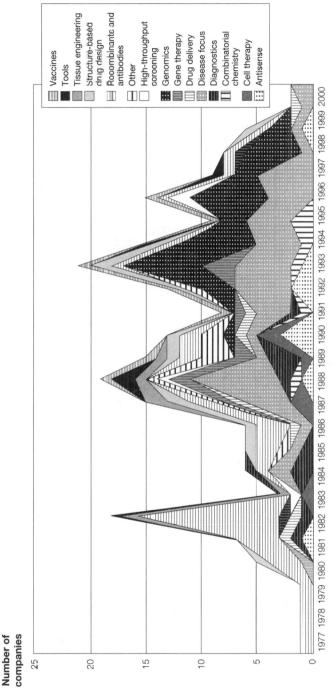

Year of founding

or Human Genome Systems, but also systems biology, as well as companies making tools for genomics research (e.g., Affymetrix). The category "disease-focused," which is the largest category, groups companies pursuing different diseases (cancer, diabetes, neurological, etc.) and even different biological approaches. Despite this lumping together of categories, the data in figure 5-2 still shows how heterogeneous the technological landscape of the biotechnology industry is. From a technological perspective, there is no one archetypal biotechnology company. The factors that may be driving this technological fragmentation are explored in detail later in this chapter.

Finally, entrants in different waves appear to be following distinct technology strategies and focusing on different technologies. The first-generation biotechnology entrants (1976–1985) focused mainly on recombinant DNA and monoclonal antibody (MAb)—large-molecule—technologies, the original genetic engineering techniques discovered in the early 1970s. The second wave of entrants, starting in the mid- to late 1980s, took a very different technological approach. They tended to focus more on specific diseases and to look to new methodologies, such as structure-based drug design, to discover traditional small-molecule chemical synthesized drugs. Finally, the early to mid-1990s witnessed the beginning of the "genomics" wave. These changes in technology strategy reflect that changes in the scientific environment shaped commercial R&D strategies, but they are also related to changes in assumptions about appropriate business models for the sector. The evolution of these business models and technology strategies is discussed below.

First-Generation Biotech:
Large Molecules and FIPCOs

Genentech's founding in 1976 marked the beginning of the first biotech wave. First-generation entrants pursued technology strategies that reflected the scientific landscape at the time. Like Genentech, other first-generation entrants pursued a technology strategy of applying the relatively new tools of rDNA and MAb technology to drug discovery.

The formation of Genentech is important for several reasons. The most obvious is that Genentech was the first commercial firm to be formed to exploit the commercial potential of the genetic engineering science. Its formation, and its wildly successful initial public offering in 1980,[3] created an enormous stimulus for other new entrants, including Amgen, Biogen, Chiron, Cetus, Genetics Institute, and Genzyme.

Not only did Genentech establish a kind of proof of *business* concept, its scientific work laid critical foundations for the application of rDNA technology to drug development. For example, in 1977 Genentech produced the first cloned human protein, somatostatin, in a bacteria cell.

Genentech's founding created a model that was followed by other early entrants. Like Genentech, they were typically founded or cofounded by university scientists—often world-renowned scientists (Biogen, for example, was cofounded by Nobel Prize winner Walter Gilbert of Harvard in 1980). The early entrants also maintained extremely close links to universities, often licensing some of their basic technology from the labs of their cofounders and working closely with faculty and postdocs on research projects. Boyer actually retained his full-time professorship at UCSF but consulted for Genentech and played a critical role in directing its research. In many cases, the first-generation biotech companies began life as "virtual enterprises," with no physical assets and few full-time employees. Until 1978 Genentech had no laboratories of its own. Its entire R&D was conducted through contracts with researchers at such academic centers as University of California, San Francisco, and the City of Hope Medical Center in Duarte, California.[4]

Perhaps most critically, Genentech pioneered an entirely new business model for entrants into the pharmaceutical industry. Historically, one of the chief barriers to entry into pharmaceuticals was the relatively high costs of R&D and long time horizons for putting a drug on the market. In the mid-1970s, a new entrant would need to be able to fund an R&D investment of approximately $300 million (in 1970s dollars) over ten to twelve years to put its first drug on the market.[5] At the time, there were simply no viable funding mechanisms available for long-term, high fixed-costs investments. It is no wonder that venture capitalists in the United States during the 1960s and 1970s preferred to focus their attention and capital on electronics companies rather than pharmaceutical companies. Genentech and the other new entrants into the biotechnology field, of course, faced the same barriers to entry.

The critical business innovation made by Genentech was to enter an R&D agreement with a major pharmaceutical company, Eli Lilly, to fund the development of its recombinant insulin program. This agreement, signed on August 25, 1978 (about eighteen months into the life of Genentech), called for Eli Lilly to fund Genentech's continued development of recombinant insulin in return for worldwide manufacturing and marketing rights to the product made with Genentech's technique. Genentech would also receive royalties on future product sales made by Lilly.[6]

What was so important about this agreement? After all, there is nothing particularly innovative about business contracts. They have existed in various forms for centuries. The Genentech-Lilly agreement, however, created a template that influenced the evolution of the biopharmaceutical industry for the next thirty years. Throughout the postwar period, the pharmaceutical industry was highly vertically integrated from R&D through marketing. Companies largely relied on their internal R&D laboratories to generate their own product candidates. Licensing of compounds in development occurred, but it was generally done between U.S. and foreign pharmaceutical companies for market access. In some instances it was done when firms inadvertently discovered compounds outside their marketing scope. When pharmaceutical companies did fund R&D at external sources, these almost always took the form of sponsored research agreements with universities or specialized technical consulting. The Genentech-Lilly agreement represents the first time that a pharmaceutical company essentially conducted a proprietary R&D program through collaboration with an external for-profit enterprise.

The agreement also provided a proof of feasibility of R&D collaboration as a mode of funding. The model was quickly emulated by other new entrants. The Genentech-Lilly agreement was the first transaction in what became a burgeoning market for know-how with young start-ups (like Genentech) on the supply side and established pharmaceutical companies (like Lilly) on the demand side. The available data suggests that these collaborations became fairly ubiquitous and quite important for young biotech entrants. For instance, between 1976 and 1980, revenues from R&D contracts funded approximately 70 percent of Genentech's total costs and expenses.[7] Virtually every new entrant into the emerging biotechnology field formed at least one, and usually several, contractual relationships with established pharmaceutical (and sometimes chemical) companies. While the specific contractual form of these arrangements varied dramatically,[8] the basic concept was the same. The established corporate partner provided funding (usually for specific R&D programs) in exchange for a license to further develop and commercialize the resulting products. These collaborations and the market for know-how became vehicles for young biotechnology firms to monetize intellectual property.

A second feature of first-generation biotech firms was their R&D strategy of using the techniques of genetic engineering as a technology platform to discover and develop a broad range of products. Genentech quickly broadened its research portfolio to include an array of products. Its first annual report (1980) disclosed R&D programs in insulin (with Lilly), growth hormone (with Kabi Vitrum), thymosin alpha-1, leukocyte and fibroblast interferon (with Roche), and bovine growth hormone (with Monsanto). By 1984 the company's R&D portfolio had expanded significantly to include a broader range of therapeutic areas (tissue plasminogen activase; alpha-, beta-, and gamma-interferons; tumor necrosis factor; and factor VIII), animal health products (e.g., a foot-and-mouth disease vaccine), enzymes for food, chemical, and consumer applications (via a joint venture with Corning), instrumentation (in collaboration with Hewlett-Packard), and diagnostics (in collaboration with Baxter-Travenol). A similar strategy of leveraging genetic engineering techniques across a broad spectrum of applications and markets could be seen in companies like Amgen, Biogen, Cetus, and others.

Both elements of the initial business models—collaboration and pursuit of broad applications—began to change shortly after 1980. Genentech's successful initial public offering in 1980 changed the context in which biotechnology firms operated. The effect of the event was far more significant than the $35 million raised in the offering. Genentech's IPO demonstrated that a firm without product revenues could raise money in public equity markets, which opened a whole new source of capital and made it possible, from a financial point of view, to contemplate vertical integration. The apparent availability of large amounts of capital from public equity markets meant that collaboration was no longer the only route to entry. Now, with public equity money available, young biotechnology companies— often with little or no development—announced aspirations to become fully integrated pharmaceutical companies, or FIPCOs, in the jargon that became popular at the time.

Second-Generation Entrants: Reintegrating Chemistry

Many in the industry initially believed that biotechnology provided a relatively low-risk approach to development. Because biotech products were proteins found in the human body, it was widely believed (or at least argued) by scientists, management, and Wall Street that biotechnology-based drugs would have a much lower failure rate than conventional, chemical-based drugs. After all, the thinking went, the proteins derived from genetic engineering were already naturally present in the body. The presumption was that these biotech protein drugs would at least be less risky to develop. The lower technological risks meant lower business risks. As companies and investors began to learn, however, this assumption was precarious.

First-generation biotech drug discovery efforts could be divided into three main types of drugs: replacement hormones, novel recombinant proteins, and monoclonal antibodies. *Replacement hormones* are substances like insulin, growth factor, and Factor VIII, which were already on the market as drugs long before biotech. As noted in chapter 2, before biotech, they were produced from culturing natural sources (e.g., pig pancreases, in the case of insulin). Biotech versions of these drugs altered the production process but kept the final product largely the same. For replacement hormones, the assumptions discussed above were valid. Insulin, for instance, had been in use since the early 1920s and scientists understood exactly what it did in the body and how it worked. Recombinant versions of these products were not expected to change the clinical profile appreciably. The initial success of a few genetically engineered replacement hormones such as insulin, human growth hormone, and Factor VIII only helped to fuel the belief that biotech drugs in general would be less risky from both a clinical and development risk point of view.

Novel recombinant proteins are proteins never before been used as drugs but suspected (based on previous biomedical research) to have desirable therapeutic effects. The vast majority of first-generation biotech R&D projects would have fallen into this category, which would have included proteins like the interferons (alpha, beta, gamma), interleukin-2 (Il-2), tissue plasminogen activase, and erythropoietin. At the time, the press was full of accounts of the promise of these wonderful substances. Interferons were widely touted for their immune-boosting effects and as a huge breakthrough against cancer. Interleukin-2 was on the cover of *Fortune* magazine on November 25, 1985, and described in an article as a "cancer breakthrough."[9] The problem was that before genetic engineering no one could produce enough of these substances to conduct much scientific research on their therapeutic uses. In reality, most of these proteins had only been studied in extremely limited laboratory (animal) investigations. As a result, biologically, these proteins were quite different from the replacement hormones described above. They were far from being "no-brainers." Scientific knowledge about what they did, and how they worked, was in fact quite limited.

This uncertainty played itself out in clinical development. While some of these proteins—like erythropoietin, G-CSF, and tissue plasminogen activase—proved themselves in the clinic, many others faced a more tortuous and tortured clinical path. Interferons caused nasty side effects (fevers, chills, etc.) and showed little promise against most cancers. In fact, alpha-interferon was initially approved for just one type of cancer—hairy cell leukemia. Some years later, alpha-interferon found its first major therapeutic score against multiple sclerosis. Il-2 also proved to be far less effective than anticipated against most cancers and also had troubling side effects.

Perhaps most disappointing in the early period were the clinical results from the third class of biotech drugs—*monoclonal antibodies* (MAbs). Touted as "magic bullets" because of their ability to bind very specifically to an antigen surface, they could, the theory went, deliver any drug to a diseased cell without harming healthy cells.

However, as a slew of these drugs marched through clinical trials, their Achilles' heel was exposed: because they were derived from murine (mouse) cells, the human body's immune system saw them as invaders and triggered a strong response, resulting in severe side effects and limiting the efficacy of the drugs themselves. While mouse-derived monoclonals found success in diagnostic kits, they were, by and large, a failure as drugs. It was not until Genentech discovered a method to "humanize" MAbs in 1990 that the technology began to realize its promise in human therapeutics.

As the reality of the risks associated with biotech drug development began to sink in, investors became much less enamored with the FIPCO strategy. By about the mid-1980s, it was beginning to lose favor on Wall Street. Even the largest, best-capitalized public biotechnology companies at the time had only enough resources to fund a very limited number of drug development programs without a corporate partner. The fortunes of many companies rested on the success of a single project. And when those projects failed in the clinic, as they did for Cetus with Il-2, the consequences were dire.[10]

A better appreciation of the realities of rDNA and MAb drug development, along with growing skepticism about the desirability of the FIPCO strategy, influenced the second wave of biotechnology entrants. As seen in figure 5-2, this second generation of entrants pursued a greater variety of technology strategies than first. Gene therapy, cell therapy, tissue engineering, and antisense emerge on the commercial scene during this phase. However, the single biggest category of new entrants during this time period was companies that focused on specific diseases (e.g., cancer, neurological disorders), specific disease mechanisms (e.g., inflammation, angiogenesis), or even specific disease targets. Very often, these new entrants grew out of the research conducted by university (and medical school) academics on the biology of specific diseases (e.g., cancer biology). The assumption behind the disease-focused strategy was that deeper biological knowledge of the underlying disease would enable the firm to more effectively and efficiently discover drugs. Whereas first-generation biotech firms were consciously "antichemistry" in their outlook, second-generation biotech entrants were much more willing to embrace small molecules as a mode of treatment.

These second-generation biotechnology entrants also pursued a different business model than their predecessors. Rather than aspiring to become fully integrated pharmaceutical companies, second-generation entrants adopted an explicit strategy of focusing their efforts on research and collaborating with established pharmaceutical companies on development and commercialization. The revenue model was based on up-front payments, milestone (progress) payments, and back-end royalties on sales. The appeal of the partner-driven strategy was that it allowed the entrant to specialize in the stage of the R&D process—early research—where small companies were supposed to have a comparative advantage over larger pharmaceutical corporations. It was also a less risky strategy because the new entrant could broaden its R&D portfolio across a broad range of programs and partners. Another factor driving this model was the technology acquisition strategies of larger pharmaceutical companies (the buy side of the market for know-how). While in the earliest days of biotechnology, pharmaceutical companies were willing to underwrite biotechnology firm R&D programs at very early stages of development, their tolerance for the risks associated with this approach began to narrow. By the late 1980s and early 1990s, most pharmaceutical companies began to look for in-licensing opportunities of programs that were either in late stages of preclinical development or early stages of human clinical testing (e.g., Phase 1) trials. It was no longer enough to have a concept. The market for know-how wanted molecules, not concepts.

Third-Generation Biotechnology: Genomics, Platforms, and the "Industrialization of R&D"

In 1990 the National Institutes of Health (NIH) and the Department of Energy (DOE) launched the Human Genome Project—an international effort to create a complete "map" of all the genes contained in human cells. When the project was launched with $3 billion in government funding, the expected target completion date was 2005. The belief was that such a map, once created, would be of enormous value to researchers searching for causes and treatments of disease. The Human Genome Project marked a watershed in biology research, not just because of its (then) audacious goal, but because of the fundamentally new research process it adopted. Historically, both biology research and drug research were undertaken with relatively labor-intensive craftlike processes. Biologists tested one hypothesis at a time. Medicinal chemists skillfully synthesized molecules by hand and then carefully screened these, one at a time, against known disease targets. The Human Genome Project ushered in the era of a new research paradigm that revolved around high-speed automation and the analysis of massive quantities of data. Software engineering, computational horsepower, and equipment design became as important as, if not more important than, the hand of the skilled bench scientist. Thus was born the era of "industrialized" drug R&D.

The premise behind industrialized drug R&D was that with the massive amount of biological data produced by the sequencing of the human genome, the craft-based, one-molecule-at-a-time approach to drug discovery would be untenable and ultimately obsolete. Industrialized R&D—the simultaneous application of genomics, bioinformatics, high throughput screening (HTS), and combinatorial chemistry—would not only transform drug R&D, but also lead to massive gains in drug R&D productivity.

While the anticipated scientific payoffs might have been a decade or more away, the advent of industrialized R&D had a profound impact on the biotechnology commercial landscape. Both venture capital and public equity markets responded with enthusiasm. Two types of companies made up the genomics wave. One group of companies—including Applied Biosystems and Affymetrix—focused on providing the tools needed for genomics research or for using genomics in drug discovery (e.g., DNA sequencers, gene chips). Another group—Celera, Incyte, Human Genome Sciences, Millennium Pharmaceuticals, and others—directly undertook genomics research.

Many of the new entrants in this third wave based their strategies on specific technology platforms (e.g., genomics or HTS) rather than specific product technologies or therapeutic applications. Yet companies adopted a different model. They would sell access (through licenses or subscriptions) to their core platform to a broad range of prospective clients and partners for different therapeutic applications. For instance, companies specializing in developing large proprietary genomic databases (such as Incyte, Human Genome Sciences, and Celera) sought to earn revenue through subscriptions. Other companies, such as Millennium, pursued a strategy of using proprietary database and genomic research tools to discover novel targets for drug discovery and then selling these targets to larger pharmaceutical companies. What was different about the platform business models was that the collaborations generally did not involve product development; rather, they focused on "inputs" into the drug discovery process: data, tools, or specific disease targets.

The fundamental economic premise behind the platform strategy was also different. Whereas earlier generations of entrants tried to capture as much value as possible on specific drugs (e.g., 100 percent for the FIPCO model), the platform business model was predicated on the idea of getting a small slice of a very broad cross-section of drugs. As expressed in a common adage among venture capitalists, it is better to get 1 percent royalties on $200 billion in product sales, than 100 percent of the profits from a billion-dollar drug.

As with previous waves, the genomics wave was initially greeted with a high degree of promise and investor enthusiasm. And, as with previous waves, experience (or perhaps just better disclosure) shed new light on the cold scientific realities. Predictions that genomics would *ultimately* transform the process and economics of drug R&D were and are well founded. Few in the scientific community doubt that more precise understanding of the genetic underpinnings of disease will lead to enormous progress in therapeutics. Where predictions were wildly optimistic (and perhaps "hyped") had to do with timing of impact. Expectations that genomics would have a short-term impact on drug R&D productivity were unfounded. As the full sequencing of the human genome neared completion, a new reality began to set in for investors: the sequencing of the human genome was just the beginning. Perhaps the biggest surprise of the genome project was that the total number of human genes was much smaller than originally anticipated. This meant that there were likely to be very few one-gene diseases. It also implied that understanding the complex interactions between genes and the enormously complex proteins they produced was essential to the search for drugs. The genome provided structural information on genes, but there was precious little knowledge about the biological function of most genes. What proteins did they code? What did those proteins do biologically? How did they interact with other proteins in disease processes? Like most important and interesting science projects, the Human Genome Project identified the next important and interesting *scientific* questions to ask. It was outstanding science, but in the short term, at least, it did not appear to be a business.

A similar skepticism began to arise regarding the overall promise of "industrialized" pharmaceutical R&D. The idea behind industrialized R&D was that by applying a combination of genomics, combinatorial chemistry, HTS, and information technology, companies could dramatically improve the rate of drug discovery. No longer would scientists working in isolated small teams have to conduct one experiment at a time on a specific molecule or therapeutic target. With industrialized R&D, a laboratory running 24/7 could generate and test millions of molecules in untold combinations against thousands of targets. Biological insight was to have given way to the law of large numbers.

While it is true that combinatorial chemistry increased the *quantity* of chemical entities vastly, it seems to have had little effect on the *quality* of compounds. The number of clinical compounds (i.e., compounds that make it to human clinical testing) has not increased markedly since the advent of industrialized R&D (see figure 5-3).

This could be due to many causes, and it by no means condemns the industrialized approach. However, accounts from the industry also suggest that industrialized R&D has been disappointing. For instance, combinatorial chemistry was initially expected to increase the productivity of discovery chemistry (through automation) by orders of magnitude. Combinatorial chemistry did not turn out to be a panacea for drug discovery. According to a study by David Newman of the National Cancer Institute, combinatorial chemistry methods had failed to produce a single FDA-approved drug by the end of 2002.[11] A big part of the problem is that combinatorial chemistry "mindlessly" creates compounds without regard to the structural characteristics that make a molecule suitable as a drug. For a compound to be a drug, it needs to be biologically active—that is, have the ability to bind to a target of interest—and pharmacologically suitable—that is, have a form that can be absorbed and metabolized appropriately. To find a good drug, therefore, you *need* biological and pharmacological knowledge. And this knowledge was lacking in combinatorial chemistry. While combinatorial chemistry produced mil-

FIGURE 5-3

Number of INDs filed, 1986–2004

Number
of INDs

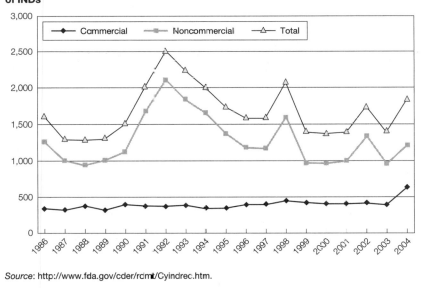

Source: http://www.fda.gov/cder/rdmt/Cyindrec.htm.

lions of compounds quickly (as advertised), its products were too often biologically inert and pharmacologically intractable.

As the genomics wave of entry came to an end, a change also began to take place in the business models of the existing genomics entrants. As noted above, most of the genomics entrants pursued a platform business model: rather than trying to develop specific drugs themselves, they would make enabling technology available (through a license, service fees, or subscription) to companies in the business of drug R&D. Thus companies like Millennium could leverage their genomic-target identification platform by striking lucrative agreements to supply large numbers of drug targets to their pharmaceutical company partners. Companies like Celera and Human Genome Sciences offered access to their genomics databases by subscription. By about 2001, however, the platform business model was, at least publicly, being called into question by these very same firms. Millennium announced that it would vertically integrate forward into drug R&D (and acquired Core Therapeutics, which had a drug already on the market). Celera and HGS, too, vertically integrated in product R&D. They would not just sell their genomics data; rather, they would use that data themselves to develop drugs and diagnostics. Vertical integration, the model aspired to by first-generation entrants twenty years before, was once again the strategy of choice. In terms of business models, the industry had gone full circle.

It is hard to identify precisely the underlying causes for the evolution in business models in the biotech sector. Wall Street perceptions and certainly fads may have played some role. As noted earlier, in the case of FIPCOs, once Wall Street was exposed to the risk of the strategy, investors quickly soured on it, and firms were quick to adjust their stated aspirations. A similar phenomenon occurred with genomics. By 2001 companies that used terms like "tools" and "platform" to describe their business models were shunned by venture capitalists and analysts. Product companies once again became kings. Ironically, while the term FIPCO was not used, firms following an essentially FIPCO strategy were being embraced.

In the case of genomics, the situation is complicated by the equity bubble that developed in the late 1990s. Platform strategies might have been perfectly economically viable at specific equity valuations. However, soaring valuations in essence raised the bar for companies' revenue models. What was a perfectly viable business model at a $2 billion equity valuation was no longer viable at a $20 billion valuation. Moreover, the enormous amounts of capital involved not only raised the bar on earnings, but also changed the firm's strategic options. As with first-generation FIPCOs, a generous equity market made it possible to raise enough funds to vertically integrate forward.

EVOLUTION OF FIRM
CAPABILITIES OVER TIME

The discussion of entry patterns illustrates that, in aggregate, the capabilities of the biotech sector have evolved over time. At different junctures, entrants with distinct R&D strategies and technical capabilities entered the industry. There also appears to have been some degree of vertical capability broadening. This section addresses the question of how technological capabilities evolved at the firm level: Did technically specialized firms broaden the scope of their R&D capabilities over time? Did their internal technological strategies reflect the changes in the external technological environment over time?

One way to glean insight about companies' internal R&D capabilities and strategies is to look at their patenting patterns. Perhaps the best study of patents in the biotechnology sector was conducted by Jesper Sorensen and Toby Stuart.[12] For a sample of 237 firms, Sorensen and Stuart examined how firm age influences the tendency of firms to innovate further outside their initial competences. One way to investigate this is to examine a firm's patent citations. When a patent is filed, the inventor is required to cite the other patents that the current invention builds on. Research has shown that citations are a reasonable proxy for where firms look for ideas. Sorensen and Stuart found that as biotechnology firms age, they tend to cite (disproportionately) more of their own patents than those of other biotechnology firms; that is, they tend to build on their own previous work. Rather than responding to the broadening technological environment they faced, it appears that biotechnology firms become more inward-looking with age.

Another way to look at the problem is to examine the nature of companies' R&D projects in different phases of development. While the "pipeline" as it looks at one point in time is, at some level, a static picture, we can assume that projects at different clinical phases were initiated at different points in time. Thus the products already on the market reflect the company's R&D strategy eight to twelve years ago. On the other hand, the projects in early phases of clinical development reflect choices made more recently. The most interesting companies to examine in this way are the oldest biotechnology companies, which entered during the first wave, with focused technological capabilities (rDNA and/or MAb). These companies have been around the longest and have had the most opportunities to expand their technological boundaries. Figures 5-4(a) and 5-4(b) offer a snapshot of the development pipelines of two biotech pioneers—Amgen and Genentech, respectively—as of 2004.

FIGURE 5-4(a)

Amgen's pipeline

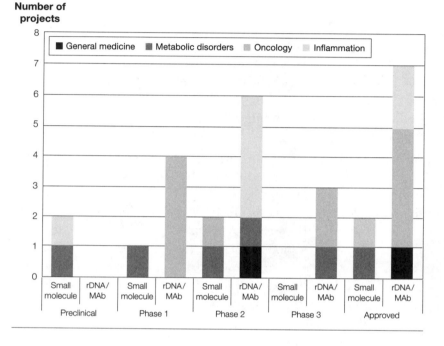

One might expect Amgen and Genentech, as the two largest, and two of the most mature, biotech firms, to have had the best opportunity to diversify their R&D portfolios over time. The projects are categorized according to current stage of development, core technology ("large molecule" versus "small molecule"), and therapeutic indication. These data were obtained from the annual reports and Web sites of both firms and are thus limited to publicly disclosed projects. Products or projects were counted only once within each broad therapeutic indication, though a product could be counted more than once if it was being developed for multiple indications.

These detailed profiles of Amgen and Genentech are generally consistent with the findings of Sorensen and Stuart. A look at the Amgen pipeline makes it clear that the company has focused its R&D strategy on four major therapeutic areas—oncology, inflammation, general medicine, and metabolic disorders. The firm's early focus on

FIGURE 5-4(b)

Genentech's pipeline

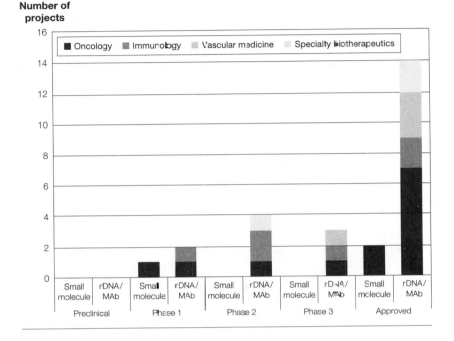

large molecules is also evident; the vast majority of its existing products and development projects are based on either rDNA or MAb technology. A shift toward small molecules is evident only in the earliest stages of the pipeline. Genentech's strategy appears even more focused on large molecules; the firm does not appear to be increasing its emphasis on small molecules even in its early pipeline.

How can we explain the lack of technological breadth among the oldest players in the industry? There are several possible explanations. First, as argued by Sorensen and Stuart (and other organizational theorists), there may be organizational processes at work that foster inertia: organizations tend to do what they are already doing. They develop internal processes and structures that favor existing technology. Second, to the extent that these processes and structures are specialized (to the existing technology), broadening the technology base could be quite costly, requiring the hiring of new people and investment in new assets—the manufacturing plants and processes used to produce chemical drugs differ entirely from those used to produce biologics. Focusing technological effort enables firms to leverage existing investments in knowledge, infrastructure, and people. Finally, to the extent that competence is enhanced by experience, companies may also deem it in their best strategic interest to focus on their unique core. Relatively few companies, for instance, are capable of developing processes and executing production for rDNA and MAb biologics. Thus first-generation pioneers, like Amgen and Genentech, have a competitive advantage in this technology. Moving into small molecules would put them into direct competition with large pharmaceutical companies that have been developing and manufacturing chemically synthesized drugs for fifty years or more.

Whether a focused technology strategy will be best in the longer term for any individual firm is difficult to know at this point. Being too focused is clearly risky, particularly if much better technological opportunities arise in other domains. However, the focused strategy of biotech entrants has resulted in a sector that contains a relatively broad diversity of technological strategies. That is, the diverse technological environment is mirrored by the diverse technological strategies of individual firms. Convergence of R&D strategies has not yet occurred in biotechnology.

LARGE PHARMACEUTICAL COMPANIES
AND THE MARKET FOR KNOW-HOW

It is impossible to understand the history and evolution of the biotech business without considering the role of large, established pharmaceutical companies that dominated the industry since the 1940s. The biotech business is not just a story of biotech firms. Major pharmaceutical companies have played a role both as direct participants in the R&D as well as through their numerous alliances with young biotech firms. Like their biotech counterparts, the strategies of major pharmaceutical firms evolved over time with changes in the technological landscape.

We can think of the technology strategies of major pharmaceutical companies in three dimensions. One is the choice of therapeutic markets (cardiovascular, cancer, etc.). Most major pharmaceutical companies now pursue a relatively broadly diversified portfolio of therapeutic markets. Research by Rebecca Henderson and Ian Cockburn provides a rationale for this diversification. They found significant scope economies in pharmaceutical R&D; that is, knowledge and capabilities accumulated in the pursuit of one therapeutic area can often be leveraged to others.[13]

The second dimension defines the choice of technologies for drug R&D (e.g., rDNA, MAb, combinatorial chemistry, genomics, rational drug design). There is a common perception that major pharmaceutical companies are not pursuing novel approaches to drug discovery. This is by and large not true, at least by around 2000. It may have been true that many pharmaceutical firms lagged in their investments and interest in novel approaches initially, but almost all major pharmaceutical companies (the top five to ten globally) have established internal R&D programs in some combination of the novel drug science technologies (such as genomics). The signs of this commitment can be gleaned from decisions firms make about where to locate research facilities and whom to hire for senior research positions.[14]

The third dimension concerns the source of projects: in-house R&D generated versus in-licensed or otherwise externally acquired. Again, there is a common misperception that pharmaceutical firms today do very little in-house R&D and rely heavily on young biotech firms for their new ideas and projects. While it is true that major pharmaceutical firms have rapidly increased their technology and drug in-licensing, it would be untrue to say that they do not perform internal research or that they leave all the breakthrough research to their smaller biotech firm partners.

Unfortunately, precise data on breakdown between in-house and external R&D is not consistently available over time. Furthermore, definitions about what constitutes "outside" spending vary—for example, is an equity investment counted as outside R&D? A glimpse of the trend toward more external R&D is provided by a survey conducted by the Pharmaceutical Research and Manufacturers of America in

2002.[15] This survey (of PhRMA members) indicated that in 1993 pharmaceutical companies spent 23 percent of their R&D on various outside sources. This figure climbed to 28 percent in 1997 and was reported to be 31 percent in 1998. Unfortunately, there does not appear to be any comparable data subsequent to that year.

Another way to understand the role of external R&D—not strictly comparable with the above—is to examine the relative percentage of drug development candidates in-licensed from external sources (versus produced internally). In 2002 the top ten largest pharmaceutical companies (ranked by number of projects in development) collectively in-licensed 47 percent of their drug development candidates.[16] There was some variation across firms, with the lowest being 43 percent and the highest being 55 percent. Extending the sample to the top twenty companies drops the figure to 43 percent. But going all the way to the top fifty drops the figure to only 41 percent. It thus appears that a fairly substantial number of drug candidates developed by the world's largest pharmaceutical companies come from some external source (a university, a smaller biotech company, or another large pharmaceutical company). Nevertheless, the majority of projects continues to be generated internally. Whether this continues to be true in the future is a matter of some speculation and will depend on the R&D strategies of major companies, an issue we turn to later in the book.

Nor is it true that the big pharmaceuticals firms are obtaining their most technologically or scientifically advanced projects from alliance partners. Ilan Guedj's recent study of 4,057 pharmaceutical projects conducted by forty large pharmaceutical companies between 1984 and 2001 showed no statistical difference in the novelty of drugs developed through in-house R&D as opposed to an alliance.[17] Nevertheless, alliances and licensing have been a crucial part of the anatomy of the biotech business. As mentioned earlier, new entrants have depended on alliances with major pharmaceutical companies for essential capital. No venture capitalist was willing to provide enough funding for such firms to fund their own development from early discovery all the way to the market. Their only recourse was to find partners (major pharmaceutical companies) willing to fund the development in exchange for future product rights. In essence, a market for know-how emerged as a response to a gap in the market for capital.

Emergence of a Market for Know-How

In order for a market to exist, one needs both buyers and sellers. It is easy to understand why young biotech firms were willing sellers in this market. But why were established pharmaceuticals firms willing to collaborate with biotechnology firms? Two alternative approaches might have been either to pursue the R&D themselves in-house or to collaborate directly with universities. First, it should be pointed out that these are not mutually exclusive approaches. By 2004 most major pharmaceutical companies pursued a combination of internal R&D, alliances with biotech firms, and alliances with universities.

Few established pharmaceutical companies had in-house biotechnology R&D programs prior to 1980. Monsanto, Merck, DuPont, Eli Lilly, Ciba Geigy, and Hoechst were among the few that had internal biotechnology R&D programs by 1978.[18] Recombinant DNA and MAb technology, as explained in chapter 2, represented fundamentally different methods of synthesizing drugs. The drugs from genetic engineering were large protein molecules, not the small chemically synthesized molecules that had been the bread and butter of major pharmaceutical companies for more than forty years. This technology was rooted in biology, and chemists largely dominated pharmaceutical R&D organizations. Within most established pharmaceutical companies, there was no natural scientific constituency to advocate for large-scale investment in biotechnology. Moreover, many chemists were highly skeptical of the applications of genetic engineering to drug discovery in the sector's earliest years. Protein-based drugs were a rarity, and until 1982, with the approval of recombinant insulin, the technology was largely unproven.

From a commercial standpoint, biotechnology also faced skeptics. Because protein drugs are broken down in the gut, they cannot be administered orally (e.g., in tablet form); they must be injected. This less convenient form of administration limits the use of protein drugs and was perceived at that time to dramatically limit the overall commercial potential of biotechnology. At the very least, the high level of technical and commercial uncertainty surrounding biotechnology meant that firms would probably be unwilling to commit major resources to creating large-scale internal research programs.

Collaborations with specialized companies provided a vehicle for exploring the terrain with a fairly limited and reversible commitment.

As for alliances, pharmaceutical companies could choose to collaborate with biotechnology companies and with universities. Figure 5-5 shows the total number of alliances for the top twenty pharmaceutical firms over the period 1988–2002. By and large, pharmaceutical company collaborations with biotechnology companies outnumbered their collaborations with universities.[19] The reasons for this are complex. First, in fact, pharmaceutical companies *were* establishing relationships with universities, so they were not pursuing the strategies in a mutually exclusive fashion. Lilly had an agreement with UCSF. DuPont had agreements with Caltech and Harvard. Monsanto had a relationship with the University of Washington. Hoechst had formed what was, at that time, a landmark relationship with the Massachusetts General Hospital. However, collaboration with biotechnology companies appears to have been the preferred route into this technology.

FIGURE 5-5

Total alliances for top 20 pharma companies (1988–2002)

Series 1.

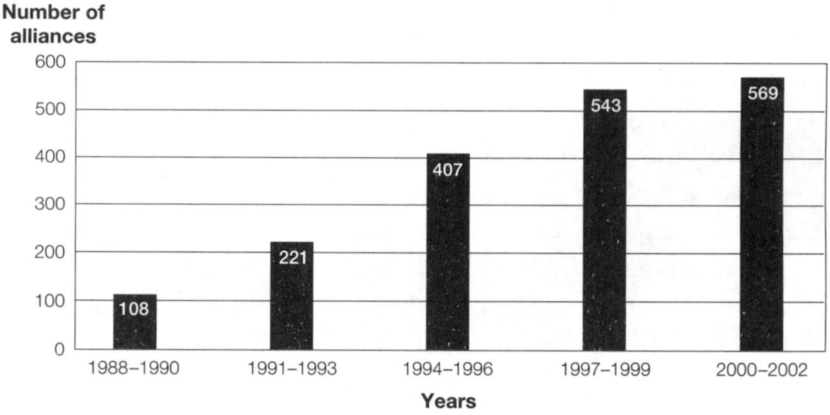

Number of alliances

Source: Recombinant Capital Source: Data adapted from Mike McCully, "How the Elephants Dance Part 4," *Signals* (www.signalsmag.com), originally published February 6, 2003.

As will be discussed in detail in chapter 7, the vast majority of biotechnology companies were spawned from intellectual property and by university scientists. Upon formation, these companies would turn around and essentially collaborate with (that is, sell their technology to) larger corporate partners. These young ventures acquired rights to technology and intellectual property from academics at a relatively early stage of development and then almost immediately sold these rights to established pharmaceutical companies.

One reason pharmaceutical companies did not go directly to universities for technology but instead went through biotech companies is that most pharma firms lacked internal capabilities to exploit the know-how on their own. The discoveries made in university laboratories, while exciting and enticing, were still in early stages and needed further development before they would be ready for clinical testing: alternative cell lines had to be explored; proteins needed to be characterized and purified; assays needed to be developed; cell culture processes had to be developed. While pharmaceutical companies had expertise in the clinical development and the regulatory process, they lacked internal scientific capabilities in these protein chemistry disciplines. At the same time, these activities were considered too "applied" for most university laboratories. Academics get rewarded for scientific breakthroughs; incremental refinements—necessary for going from scientific concept to clinical drug—are not the stuff of which academic careers are made. Thus biotechnology firms filled the gap between basic scientific discovery and applied development. Most of the R&D done by biotechnology firms was too applied for a university setting, but too early-stage for most pharmaceutical companies. Until they built up their own internal capabilities, pharmaceutical companies needed to collaborate with biotechnology firms for bridging this gap.

There were exceptions to the above patterns. Eli Lilly was an early mover in biotechnology. It had an internal research program established in the late 1970s due to its long history (and enormous commercial interests) in producing insulin—a protein produced through biological means. Merck had a long history of attracting top academic and scientific talent to its internal laboratories (largely in the area of medicinal chemistry). Monsanto initiated cell biology research (for agricultural applications) in 1973.[20] Other major companies were able to recruit top scientific talent and forge links with universities. Nevertheless, the basic pattern described above is accurate; young biotechnology firms spawned from universities were the dominant locus of biotechnology R&D in the early stages of the sector's life. They had the closest relationship with universities, often physically colocated inside university laboratories (in their very first days) or located nearby. Established pharmaceutical companies mainly accessed technology through collaborative relationships with these firms.

Evolution of the Market for Know-How

The market for know-how in biotechnology has evolved in at least three ways. Figure 5-5 shows the total number of alliances between established pharmaceutical companies and biotechnology companies between 1988 and 2002. At a very crude level, the market for know-how has become much larger. Part of this growth reflects the simple fact that the number of biotechnology firms has grown dramatically, thus expanding the potential supply of partnered projects. Growth in alliances has also been fueled by pharmaceutical companies' strategies mentioned above to look outside their own laboratories for R&D. While the propensity to collaborate with biotechnology firms varies across major pharmaceutical companies, virtually all companies today are involved in at least several major alliances.

Evolution has also occurred with respect to the nature of projects being undertaken collaboratively, and specifically, the R&D stage at which collaboration commences. Because the pharmaceutical R&D process is a long one, it presents a wide path of choice for the timing of collaboration within the development cycle. Figure 5-6 provides a picture of how the timing of collaboration has varied over the life of the biotechnology industry. Note that this analysis was limited to only those alliances for which the stage of signing was reported in the Recombinant Capital database (about 50 percent of the projects). Nevertheless, this still provides a reasonable picture of how the timing of partnering has changed over time.

It is often assumed that large pharmaceutical companies are only interested in licensing in later-stage projects, where the remaining development risks are lower. This is not born out by the data. Between 1998 and 2002, deals struck at the discovery stage—the

FIGURE 5-6

Timing of collaboration within the development cycle

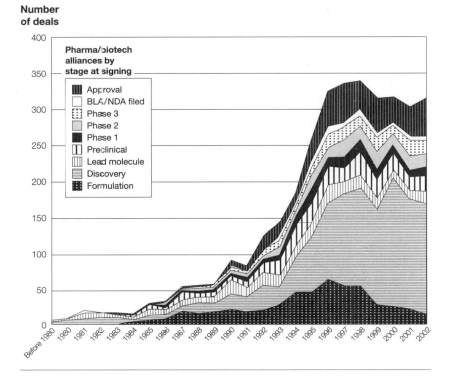

earliest stage of the process—account for an average of 48 percent of the alliances between biotechnology firms and pharmaceutical firms. It is true that over time the share of later-stage deals has grown, but this may simply reflect the shifting overall demographics of the industry's R&D portfolio. In the earliest years of the industry, its total portfolio contained relatively few late-stage projects. As the industry matured and as projects made their way through the development process, more late-stage projects became available for licensing. The market for know-how seems to be quite active across the full range of potential projects, from early-stage discovery projects to drugs that have already been approved for marketing.

The third dimension of potential evolution concerns the nature of the relationships between biotech firms and their pharmaceutical partners. How intimately are the partners related organizationally, legally, financially, and operationally? We can think of these relationships along a continuum. At one end of the spectrum—the least intimate end—are *arm's-length* contractual arrangements. Under the arm's-length agreements, there is very little organizational, legal, financial, or operational integration. The terms of trade are spelled out in a contract. Each party remains highly independent, and the only concern is whether the terms of trade are met. Short-term R&D contracts, licensing agreements, and fee-for-service agreements typically take this form. At the other end of the spectrum are very intimate collaborations that involve significant organizational, legal, financial, and operational integration. Many of these relationships involve equity investments by the pharmaceutical partners in the biotech firm (along with representation on the board of directors). Partners may agree to a long-term collaboration spanning multiple projects, and their scientists may physically colocate for some period of time. Intellectual property may be shared. Some of these relationships come very close to being outright acquisitions.

One of the interesting features of the biotechnology industry is that it contains the full range of relationships from arm's-length, fee-for-service agreements to long-term, in-depth collaborative partnerships. In an analysis of two hundred technology alliances in biotechnology struck between 1980 and 1995, Josh Lerner and Robert Merges found that the contract length (in years) varied from 0.75 years to 31 years, with a mean of 3.79 years.[21] More interesting perhaps is the variance in the rights of control in these alliances. In some cases the biotech firm originating the project retains relatively little control over the development of the drug once it collaborates with a pharmaceutical partner. But this is not universally true. In some alliances the biotech firm maintained a very high degree of control over the key decisions involving the development of the drug.

CONCLUSION

Throughout its thirty-year history, the biotechnology business has evolved in tandem with changes in the technology. Indeed, as discussed in chapter 4, when it comes to the science, there is not one "biotechnology revolution" but many. The same can be said of the business of biotechnology. Over the years, we have seen several distinct "biotechnology industries"—distinct clusters of firms pursuing specific technological and business strategies.

A few basic facts stand out. First, the technological and business strategies of firms seem to be closely associated with the epoch of entry. New waves of science drove the entry of firms specializing in and building capabilities in that science. While firms may attempt to expand their vertical boundaries, they have tended to stay relatively focused in specific technological capabilities. Even the largest and most mature biotechnology companies (e.g., Amgen, Genentech, Genzyme), for instance, are still relatively highly focused on biologics (rDNA, MAbs), despite their increasing attempts to broaden into small molecules. Using our landscape metaphor, perhaps the best way to view biotechnology is as a large group of islands of expertise. Different firms have chosen to occupy different locations on the map, as determined by their technological approaches and areas of expertise.

Yet pharmaceutical R&D requires integration. That is, one needs to access a broad constellation of technological capabilities, tools, and organizational assets. This explains another characteristic of the sector: the significant role played by collaborative arrangements. All new entrants were active sellers in the know-how market. They sought funding and access to markets via collaboration with established pharmaceutical companies. Yet collaborative models have not been the "equilibrium form." Most companies, over time, have attempted to vertically integrate forward; that is, they have tried to develop and market their own drugs rather than license them out.

The picture portrayed in this chapter is one of a sector containing a wide range of technological strategies resulting from many firms each pursuing a focused approach—a sector in which alliances and collaborations among biotech firms and large, well-established pharma companies have played a crucial role; a sector that has seen a market for know-how growing over time, with an increasing number of biotech firms supplying partnered projects. Is this anatomy appropriate for the challenges the science poses? We can start to answer this question by looking at how the sector has performed over the years. This will be the focus of the next chapter.

6

The Performance
of the Biotech Industry

Promise Versus Reality

This chapter focuses on the financial and operating performance of the biotechnology industry. Throughout the history of biotech, expectations have been high. The promise of biotech was that through different (and superior) technology, the process of drug R&D would be transformed, and this transformation would lead to an avalanche of new drugs. And, of course, this would fuel profitability. In addition, it has been widely expected and perceived that smaller biotech firms are more productive at R&D than established pharmaceutical behemoths. This assumption often leads to very specific recommendations for technology strategies of pharmaceutical companies. For instance, one of the most common "words of wisdom" proffered at industry conferences is that big pharmaceutical companies should focus on marketing and leave innovative R&D to small biotech firms. This chapter explores these assumptions empirically.

FINANCIAL PERFORMANCE

Financial returns from biotech vary dramatically across firms and time, and by investment stage. An investor who was smart enough to buy a cross-section of biotechnology in 1980 and who was even smarter to sell it out in the second half of 1999 would have achieved a very attractive return. In fact, for everyone who bought in 1980 and sold in 1999, there were likely many investors who jumped into biotech during the genomics bubble. These investors wound up with small fortunes—unfortunately, they had started with much larger ones!

One simple way to look at financial returns is to consider how an investor would have done purchasing IPOs of biotech firms and holding the stock for some period of time. According to one analysis, an investor who purchased all 340 biotech IPOs between 1979 and 2000 and who held those shares until January 2001 (or until company acquisition) would have realized an average annual return of 15 percent.[1] This is by no means bad performance, but neither is it particularly stellar considering the risk inherent in biotechnology stocks (and compared to alternative, less risky investments). Another way to look at performance is to consider a hypothetical investor who purchased a diversified basket of publicly held biotechnology shares in a specific year (not just at IPO). A $1 investment in biotechnology shares in 1981 would have been worth approximately $8 at the end of 2003. This is about a 10 percent compounded rate of return. In comparison, the same investment in long-term Treasury bonds (essentially a risk-free investment) would have been worth close to $12. And the same investment in the Dow Jones would have been worth approximately $21.[2] Thus while there have been some spectacular performances in biotech (e.g., the same $1 invested in Amgen would have been worth $165), the sector, in aggregate, has yielded disappointing returns compared with alternative (generally less risky) investments.

Looking at returns on public equity gives us one perspective on performance, but it is also interesting to look at returns to private equity (venture capital), which has played such a critical role in the sector. Figure 6-1 shows the annual internal rates of return for venture capital funds focused on biotechnology.

As one might expect, rates of return for VCs in this sector are highly volatile over time, with periods of strong performance correlated

FIGURE 6-1

Annual returns for venture capital funds

AVERAGE TIME-WEIGHTED RETURNS USING PERIODIC IRRs

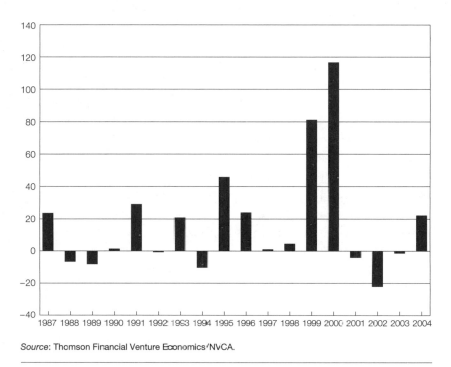

Source: Thomson Financial Venture Economics/NVCA.

closely with periods when public equity markets were most inviting new initial public offerings. There have also clearly been some periods of relatively high returns. For instance, Venture Economics reported that during the period 1996–2001, the five-year returns on venture capital funds investing at least 60 percent of their capital in biotech garnered returns of 42.5 percent.[3] This was approximately comparable to the 40 percent returns to venture capital in all sectors during the same period. However, VC returns were clearly helped greatly by the run-up in biotechnology stocks in the 1999–2001 period that opened a huge window for IPOs. If we step back and take a longer-term perspective and consider returns over the period 1986–2002, the annual internal rate of return for VC funds focused on biotech are 16.6 percent. This is just slightly better than the 15 percent returns that buyers of IPOs got over a slightly longer time horizon.

Given the presumed higher risks of venture capital investments, this performance could hardly be considered stellar.

Stock market valuation is one way to look at economic performance. Perhaps a more direct way is to simply look at the earnings of the sector. How well has it done in generating profits? An answer may be sought in a comprehensive analysis of the financial performance of every publicly held biotechnology company (see appendix A for the list of companies) in existence between 1975 and 2004. To get a sense of how well the sector as a whole has performed over its history, I created a yearly aggregate income statement for the industry. In essence, this method combines the income statements of every company, year by year since 1975, into one industry-level statement. Since earning calculations can be distorted by various kinds of accounting treatments, operating income before depreciation (cash flow) was used as the measure of profitability. This method provides a picture of how the biotech sector has performed as if it were a single firm.

Figure 6-2 shows the yearly evolution of total sector revenue and net operating income before depreciation from 1975 to 2004. The picture is striking. While revenues have grown exponentially (as we might expect in an emerging industry), profitability has been flat. Even worse, profit levels essentially hover close to zero throughout the life of the industry. Furthermore, the picture becomes even worse if we take the largest and most profitable firm, Amgen, out of the sample. Without Amgen the industry has sustained steady losses throughout its history. It should be noted that the picture provided by these data is, if anything, biased in the positive direction, for the analysis includes no privately held firms, almost all of which lose money. Therefore, the data presented here are just for the most profitable part of the industry population. Moreover, this analysis is based cash flow, not net income. Therefore, we are not taking into account depreciation, which might proxy for the costs of replacing physical capital over time.

In a sector like biotechnology, with highly skewed returns, it does not always make sense to talk about average performance. And indeed, as shown in figure 6-3, positive economic performance has been concentrated in relatively few firms. In 2004 the vast majority of publicly held biotech firms were cash-flow negative. Of the firms that

FIGURE 6-2

Biotech revenues and profitability with and without Amgen, 1975–2004*

$ millions

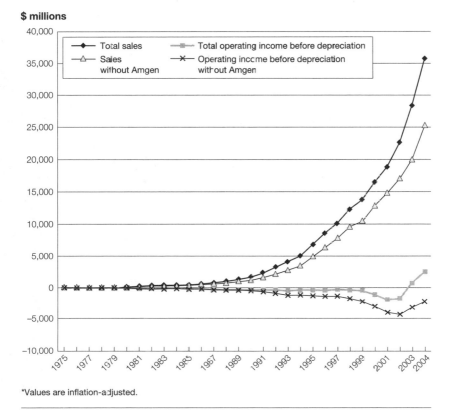

*Values are inflation-adjusted.

did generate positive cash flows, fifteen accounted for most (93 percent) of the cash generated. And two firms, Amgen and Genentech, alone accounted for more than 53 percent of the cash generated by the sector.

The next chapter begins to analyze the underlying causes of the difficult financial performance of the sector to date. Skeptics might argue that this analysis is 'unfair," in that it does not recognize the long time lags for getting new drugs to market in the industry. Granted, this is a sector with long time lags: we would not expect the

FIGURE 6-3

Biotech economic performance by firm, 2004

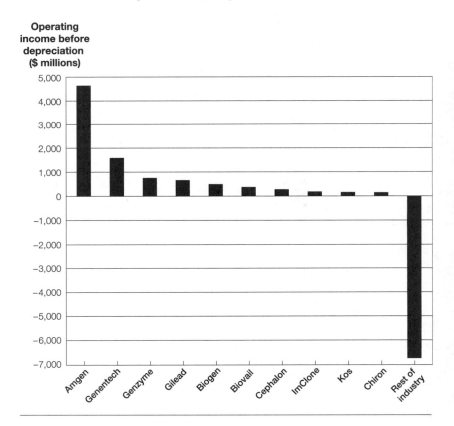

sector to generate positive profits overnight. However, a couple of points are worth noting.

First, these data span thirty years, so the time horizon covers just about two full product development cycles. Thus while we might not expect the sector to generate profits "overnight" (although optimists abounded), we might have expected better aggregate performance over a twenty-year time horizon. Second, probing underneath the sample and looking at individual firms reveals that in gross numbers, there are very few profitable biotechnology companies. The vast majority of biotechnology companies have *never* generated positive cash flows. Moreover, there are quite a few companies that have been in business for ten or more years that have never been profitable. Nor does there seem to be any evidence in the sample that profitability is simply a matter or age (i.e., given enough time, a biotech will earn profits). The average time to first year of positive cash flow (from IPO) in the sample was approximately eleven years, but some firms have been in the industry for close to twenty years without generating positive cash flows (see figure 6-4).

The issue of long lag times represents an important structural feature of this sector and is discussed in detail in subsequent chapters. It leads us to question what the appropriate funding and governance mechanisms are for firms with such unusual economic

FIGURE 6-4

Average sales and operating income following IPO

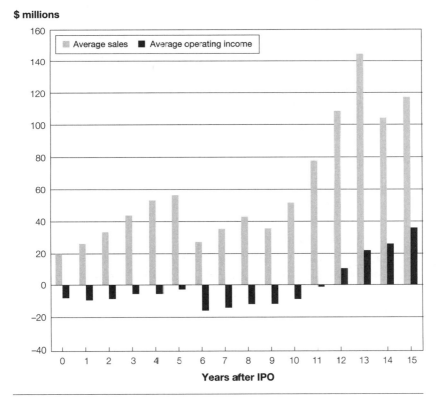

$ millions

profiles. Indeed, it is virtually impossible to find other historical examples, at least at the industry level, for which such a large fraction of new entrants can be expected to endure such prolonged periods of losses and for which the vast majority may *never* become viable economic entities.

R&D PRODUCTIVITY

Financial measures of performance give us one picture of firm and industry performance. Ultimately investors care about financial returns, and positive returns are absolutely essential for the economic viability of the industry. However, in an industry like pharmaceuticals, where R&D performance is a direct long-term driver of financial performance, R&D productivity is a good intermediate marker for performance. The ability to turn financial resources into drugs (which then drive profitability) is essential to the industry's viability.

R&D productivity has, in the last several years, become a cause for concern in pharmaceuticals. While R&D spending has increased dramatically over the past fifteen years, the rate of introduction of new drugs has not kept pace. Indeed, the rate of introduction of new chemical entities has fallen. This suggests that we are spending more but getting less—a point to which I will return. As these data predominantly pertain to the largest pharmaceutical companies, the R&D "productivity crisis" is generally viewed as a sign of weakness of big pharma. Many industry observers and analysts have concluded that biotechnology firms offer a way out of this productivity crisis. Indeed, a view that can be heard at virtually every biotech industry conference is that big pharmaceuticals would be better off focusing on marketing and outsourcing much of their R&D to small biotech companies.

This issue can be investigated by calculating the inflation-adjusted cost per new molecular entity developed by a sample of large pharmaceutical companies and a comprehensive sample of biotechnology companies—the same sample used in the financial analysis above. However, any firms from the sample that were focused only on technology platform development and never attempted to develop an actual drug are eliminated. The sample of pharmaceutical companies includes the top twenty pharmaceutical companies in the world by R&D spending. For both the biotech sample and the "big pharma" sample, we track the cumulative number of new molecular entities launched relative to the cumulative R&D spending over an eighteen-year period. Thus the measure of productivity is the (inflation-adjusted) R&D cost per new drug launched.

A few important methodological points are worth noting. First, the sample of drugs only includes new molecular entities (NMEs)—both small molecules and biologics—not line extensions, reformulations, or approvals of new indications. Second, in order to account for the lags between R&D spending and R&D output, drugs launched during the first four years of the sample period are "discounted" (down weighed) to take into account that they resulted from some spending that occurred before the sample period. An NME launched in the first year of the sample period (1984) received 10 percent credit. Launches in the second, third, and fourth years received 25 percent, 50 percent, and 75 percent credit, respectively. In addition, R&D spending during the last four years of the sample period is discounted to account for the fact that some of this R&D spending would lead to drugs that might be approved after the sample period ended. R&D spent in 2004 is weighed only 10 percent. The immediate preceding years are weighed at 25 percent, 50 percent, and 75 percent, respectively.

In addition, the effect of R&D partnerships between firms must be taken into account. This gets tricky because of the vast array of R&D collaboration structures. It is particularly problematic when a biotech firm develops a drug on its own to a certain point and then licenses it to a partner that takes over the rest of the development activities and costs. Ideally we would like to have an exact picture of the percentage of total development costs attributed to the biotech firm and the percentage accounted for by the partner. In reality, these data are not available on a consistent or comprehensive basis. Therefore a simple cost-allocation rule must suffice. For any drugs that came to market under any type of collaborative arrangement, the biotech firm originating the drug gets "credit" for half an NME and its partner gets half the credit. The same approach is applied to drugs launched by big pharmaceutical companies: if they partnered, they receive half credit.

This approach clearly has its limits. If anything, it likely penalizes large pharmaceutical companies in a couple of respects. First, existing pharmaceutical companies have a portfolio of existing drugs on the market that consume R&D resources for post-market approval studies, line extensions, development of new indications, and the development of new formulations and dosage forms. Such spending generally accounts for about 10 to 15 percent of the R&D budgets of larger pharmaceutical companies. This spending is not geared toward new molecular entity creation, and yet it is counted in the total R&D spending of the drug companies in the sample. Second, most large drug companies focus on drugs for indications with larger numbers of potential patients. Biotech firms have generally focused on more specialized markets. This generally translates into differences in the average size of clinical trials. And average number of patients in clinical trials is a major driver of R&D costs in pharmaceuticals. These caveats should be kept in mind in the interpreting of these findings.

Figure 6-5 shows the results of the analysis described above. It compares the cumulative costs per newly launched drug for the biotech sector and the pharmaceutical sector over the history of the biotech industry. As shown, there is no evidence from this data that biotech firms are any more or less productive than major pharmaceutical companies. These results do not differ markedly when we change the assumption of our model. The data shows that, in essence, after twenty years, the productivity race between established pharmaceutical companies and biotechnology is a dead heat. Given the inevitable noise in such data and the limits inherent in the methodology employed, we should not make too much of small differences. The data, despite their limits, would lead us to seriously question the hypothesis that, when it comes to R&D, biotechnology firms are significantly more productive than their large pharmaceutical counterparts. If there is a productivity problem in the industry, it seems to be equally shared by both big pharmaceutical firms and biotech firms. While expectations of an R&D productivity boom have been part of the promise of biotech, these expectations are not born out in the data, as of yet.

There are three possible criticisms of this analysis. First, one might argue that the promise of biotech is yet to come and that therefore the picture would look very different in a few years. Second, the

FIGURE 6-5

Productivity comparison of established pharmaceutical companies and biotechnology companies

CUMULATIVE R&D SPENDING PER NEW DRUG

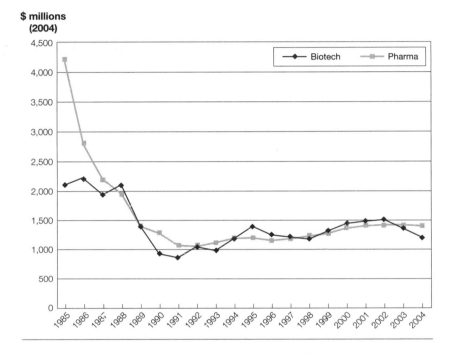

measure of output (number of drugs) is crude and does not take into account commercial potential. Finally, the measure of output does not account for differences in medical complexity or importance of the drugs. These are valid points, addressed in turn below.

The Future Will Look Different

This is, of course, an impossible hypothesis to reject, as the data will only be available in the future. However, by using a cumulative (rather than year by year) measure of productivity and lag adjustments, I hope to have dulled the potentially confounding influences of time lags. While we can never be certain that the picture will look the same (or different) in the future, projects in progress today might provide some insight on what is in store. Optimists commonly cite the fact that biotech firms account for a growing percentage of drugs in clinical development. According to some estimates, in 2003, 30 percent of the drugs in the development pipeline were biopharma-ceuticals.[4] This suggests that we should expect to see a great number of biotechnology drugs emerging from the biotech pipeline in the future. However, two important factors must be considered. First, biotechnology R&D spending continues to increase substantially. In addition, attrition rates of biotechnology drugs in development have actually been increasing over time.[5] Thus while biotech firms may have more projects in progress, it is not at all clear, given the increase in attrition rates, that their output per dollar of R&D invested will increase substantially.

Considering Revenue-Adjusted Productivity

One of the challenges of any productivity metric is to consider the relevant measure of output. In the simple analysis above, I counted drug launches, essentially weighting all drugs equally. But drugs vary dramatically in their economic impact; some drugs end up with sales of billions of dollars, while some have sales of less than $100 million. From a purely economic point of view, one might argue that output should be weighted by some measure of economic value. To explore this issue, I undertook a similar analysis as the one conducted above, but instead of counting output in terms of the number of drugs launched, I looked at total revenue generated. Again, a similar methodology of adjusting for lags was used to take into account that revenues typically lag R&D expenses by several years. And again, the results were aggregated to the sector level.

Figure 6-6 shows fairly clearly that in fact revenue per dollar of R&D is much larger for the pharmaceutical sector as a whole than for biotechnology firms. This is probably mainly due to differences in the strategic mix of products chosen by each type of firm to develop. Large pharmaceuticals typically intentionally focus on developing drugs for very large markets (e.g., hypertension, cholesterol, pain, and inflammation). For a company with, say, $40 billion in sales, achieving a target rate of growth of 10 percent requires $4 billion in incremental revenue per year. This is obviously easier to achieve by launching one

FIGURE 6-6

Revenue-adjusted productivity

BIOTECH AND PHARMA CUMULATIVE SALES PER R&D $

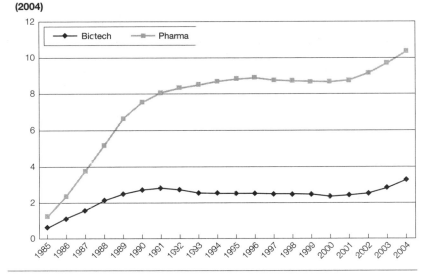

$ millions
(2004)

new blockbuster drug with expected sales of $4 billion than by launching ten new drugs each with sales of $400 million. Thus, strategically, most major pharmaceutical companies choose to focus on "big market" therapies. In contrast, biotechnology generally chooses to focus on smaller, more specialized therapies because these markets are typically easier to access. They do not require a huge army of sales representatives to call on tens of thousands of physicians' offices; they do not require large direct-to-consumer advertising budgets. Instead, more specialized markets—like cancer—can be reached with a relatively small sales force focused on a few dozen opinion leaders in the medical field. In addition, small biotech firms face a different growth imperative than the major pharmaceutical companies. For firms with *no* product revenues, introducing even a $300 million per year drug is an attractive prospect. With sales of $300 million per year, introducing another $300 million per year drug results in 100 percent growth.

Thus while the differences in sales revenue per R&D dollar invested between biotech and pharmaceutical companies is likely due largely to choice rather than "bad performance," it does underscore a problem that many industry analysts have ignored. If big pharmaceutical companies are looking to biotech to help them fill their revenue gap, these data would not make one optimistic.

Differences in Complexity, Risk, and Medical Importance

It is often argued that biotech firms undertake development projects that are somehow more complex and risky and that potentially lead to more medically important drug innovation than the projects undertaken by "big pharma." Again, simply counting drugs launched, as above, could lead one to underestimate the "true" productivity of biotech firms if these factors are at work. But are they?

This is a difficult question to answer empirically. There is no one set of criteria for judging complexity, risk, or importance. The FDA uses a priority system for approval, but in 1992, with the Prescription Drug User Fee Act (PDUFA), the system changed, making it hard to do comparisons across time. Looking only at drugs that make it to the FDA would give a distorted picture, as potentially the most innovative drugs are the also the most risky, and we might expect these drugs to have a higher attrition rate in clinical trials (i.e., they never make it to the FDA). Medical importance is also complicated. Is a drug that cures a deadly disease that afflicts a very small number of patients more or less medically important than a drug that treats a much less serious disease, impacting millions of people? It depends on one's perspective; if one has the disease, it is important.

Not surprisingly, the anecdotal evidence is mixed. Big pharmaceutical companies launch many drugs that are incremental improvements over existing drugs (so-called "me-too" drugs). But they have also launched true breakthrough drugs, including protease inhibitors for AIDS (Merck), selective serotonin re-uptake inhibitors for depression (Lilly), Tamoxifen for breast cancer (Bristol-Myers Squibb), and Gleevec for leukemia (Novartis). Biotech companies have clearly introduced a number of breakthrough drugs themselves, such as erythropoietin (Amgen) for life-threatening anemia, beta interferon for multiple sclerosis (Chiron, Biogen), a number of novel cancer treatments such as Herceptin (Genentech), and treatments for rare genetic disorders (Genzyme). But we should also keep in mind that the first-generation biotech drugs were generally not very novel therapeutically; rather, they were genetically engineered versions of drugs already on the market, but manufactured through a different process (insulin, growth hormone, Factor VIII). There is no doubt that these drugs offered benefits (e.g., purity, reduced risk of disease transmission), but they also involved comparatively lower levels of therapeutic risk.

A systematic analysis of data on drugs in development from the PharmaProjects database reveals that there is not a simple correlation between firm size and novelty of drugs in development.[6] Pharma-Projects uses its own classification scheme to identify the scientific and clinical novelty of each drug under development. The scheme takes into account whether the molecule represents a new "strategy" for treating a particular disease and how far along in the development process the drug is relative to others. The scale is a rating from 1 to 6, with 1 being least novel and or least advanced, and 6 being a leading compound. For every active project in the PharmaProjects database, I collected data on the novelty rating and the size of the firm (by market capitalization) sponsoring the project, dividing the sample of firms into categories based on size and then calculating the average novelty rating of all drugs being developed by firms in each size class. The relationship between novelty of drugs in development (measured as average novelty rating) and firm size is shown in figure 6-7.

The data show very little difference, on average, in novelty across firms in different size classes. There is a small jump in the novelty of firms in the mid-capitalization range, but this represents a fairly small increase. This data should make us skeptical that small biotech firms are systematically engaged in more innovative development than larger companies.

PRODUCTIVITY AT THE FIRM LEVEL

The analysis and discussion so far have been at the aggregate sector level, with nothing said about differences in productivity at the firm level. Yet previous research on R&D productivity suggests that

FIGURE 6-7

The relationship between firm size and drug novelty

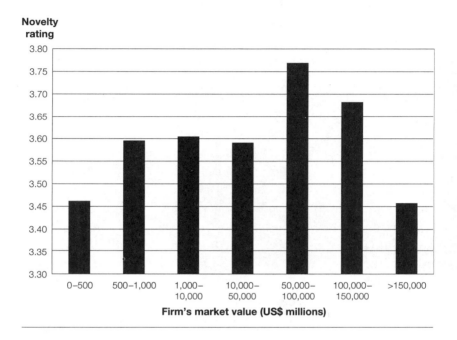

Firm's market value (US$ millions)

firm-level variation in productivity is typically quite large. To better encompass this issue, I extracted from the data the R&D performance of a subset of firms, and analyzed their productivity using a methodology similar to that described above. The choice of firms was by no means random: it comprised the five most mature biotech firms, which have had the best records of product launches (Amgen, Biogen, Chiron, Genentech, and Genzyme). Choosing mature companies minimizes the potentially negative impacts of firm start-up effects and lags on the results. For comparison, two large pharmaceutical companies—Merck and Eli Lilly—are considered as well. Merck was often considered (at least during the time frame of comparison) a bellwether for the large pharmaceutical company sector. In addition, because Merck engaged in no major mergers and acquisitions during this time frame, it is easier to get a read on its R&D performance. Lilly was chosen for similar reasons. It is among the largest pharmaceutical companies, and like Merck, it has not engaged in major M&A activity.

Figure 6-8 presents the data in a slightly different form for ease of illustration. Rather than showing a yearly running total of the R&D costs per drug, it shows data aggregated over the entire time period (1985–2004). All of the same adjustments for partnering and time lags discussed for earlier analyses were also performed here.

The data indicate a fairly high degree of variance across the companies in the cumulative R&D cost incurred per new drug launched. While this sample is not large enough to draw any kind of statistical inference about differences, the overall pattern is somewhat consistent with the aggregate analysis. The biotech firms as a group are not consistently better or worse than the big pharmaceutical company benchmarks. Some of the differences across firms may have to do with strategy. Genzyme's very low cost per new drug launched may be explained largely by its focus on developing drugs for rare genetic disorders (e.g., Gauchy's, Fabry's). Because the treatment populations for these diseases are extremely small, clinical trials tend to be much

FIGURE 6-8

R&D spending per NME, 1985–2004

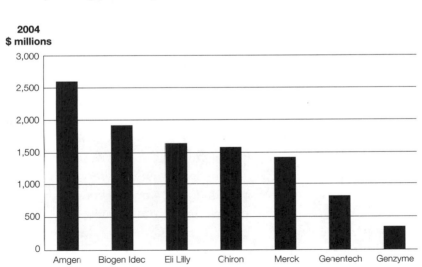

smaller in scale (and thus less costly) than the typical clinical development program. However, one should not discount the possibility that
by focusing on a very well-defined set of diseases (rare genetic diseases
that result from a missing enzyme), Genzyme has been able to also
develop and exploit unique organizational capabilities and specialized
technological know-how. Finding the right replacement enzyme, designing a clinical trial appropriate for a small patient sample, and then
actually finding and recruiting afflicted patients to participate in
the study is an extremely difficult task. While other companies have
attempted to emulate Genzymes "rare disease" business model, no one
has yet to be as successful in executing this strategy.

Genentech's comparatively low R&D cost per drug is noteworthy,
considering the firm's focus on cancer. Cancer trials tend to be long
and risky. Cancer drugs have notoriously high rates of attrition (project failure). While Genentech benefits (in this analysis) from having
launched a set of first-generation replacement proteins (insulin,
human growth hormone, Factor VIII), the company has been successful in recent years in developing innovative cancer therapeutics
such as Herceptin and Avastin.

Perhaps somewhat surprising is Amgen's relatively low performance on R&D productivity, given its extraordinary financial performance. The company launched two drugs relatively early in its
life—erythropoietin (1989) and GM-CSF (1991). These turned out
to be multibillion-dollar products that propelled Amgen's growth.
However, the company did not successfully develop another new
molecule entity on its own through the rest of the 1990s. In 2001
Amgen introduced Aransep, an improved version of EPO. In 2002
(after the sample period) Amgen acquired Immunex and the right to
Enbrel, a drug with sales of approximately $2 billion per year. The
cost of the acquisition was $16 billion.[7] Again, care should be taken
in drawing any strong conclusions from this data. While Amgen was
not successful in launching new molecular entities during the 1990s,
it invested heavily in developing and expanding the clinical profile of
both EPO and GM-CSF (i.e., gaining approval for new uses). Leveraging its core platform assets (EPO and GM-CSF) was a very successful strategy commercially.

CONCLUSION

By both financial and operational measures, the biotechnology sector has not been particularly healthy for much of its thirty-year life. Perhaps this fact is not surprising. However, it raises two interesting questions. First, how has it managed to attract capital over such a sustained period of time, given its lackluster rewards for investors? Second, what is the underlying cause of this performance?

The first question is interesting in light of the usual criticisms regarding the myopia of U.S. capital markets. We often hear that U.S. capital markets—the stock market in particular—are obsessed with the next quarter's performance. The biotech sector does not seem to fit particularly well into such an environment. Yet biotechnology firms have received the bulk of their financing from just such a market. And even more surprising, investors have tolerated years (and sometimes a decade) of losses by individual firms. Have the capital markets become lax? The evidence from other sectors suggests otherwise. Consider the Internet "bubble" of the late 1990s. There was an enormous run up in the valuations of any company with dot-com attached to its name. Yet within a relatively short time frame, once it became apparent that the vast majority of these firms had no viable business model, the capital markets pulled the plug. Venture capitalists and public investors simply stopped funding dot-coms. Sectors that do not generate positive financial returns, over the long term, cannot attract capital. Just ask an airline executive.

While biotechnology stocks are clearly volatile, the sector has shown remarkable ability to rebound and attract fresh capital, despite its poor track record. There are a few plausible explanations for this. First, while the aggregate returns to biotechnology are poor, investors are focusing on the "tails" of the distribution. The phenomenal stock market returns of a company like Amgen provide a beacon for investors. People—everyone from sophisticated VCs to Aunt Martha—invest in biotechnology companies because they hope to catch the next Amgen. Never mind that the probabilities are very low and, on a risk adjusted basis, it may not be a good bet. The promise is there.

The other force that sustains investment in the sector relates to the second issue raised above. It is often assumed that biotech has not yet reached its stride—that the industry is still in the early stages of a long-term transformation that will ultimately be very profitable. Only time will tell. However, the logic of this explanation hinges on a critical assumption: that the industry is structurally sound; that is, that it compromises the right types of firms, following the right strategies and models, influenced by the right type of institutional arrangements. If this is the case, the economics of natural selection will operate and over time (and it may take some time) a healthy set of surviving firms with robust returns will result. It is this final point that the last part of the book questions. In a nutshell, I will argue that, structurally, all is not well with biotechnology. The anatomy is not proper given the requirements of the science at this point; it does not fit. Thus simply giving biotech more time will not solve the problem. A healthy biotech sector needs to look and operate differently than the sector we see today.

7

The Monetization of
Intellectual Property

The previous two chapters examine the anatomy of the biotechnology industry (what it looks like) and its performance
until the present (how it does). We now turn to the question
of how it works: What are the underlying forces that shape the way
the industry has evolved, the way it operates, the way firms behave,
and the way various types of players interact? Without an understanding of these forces, we cannot get to the root of the performance problems. Nor can we begin to understand what might be
done to improve performance.

This chapter argues that three interrelated forces drive the business of biotechnology. Understand these, and you have a pretty good
idea of why this sector looks the way it does and why it performs the
way it does. The first is the transfer of technology from universities to
the private sector through the spawning of new firms. The second is
capital markets, including both venture capital and the public equity.
The third is the market for know-how in which younger ventures
trade intellectual property (IP) for funding through various forms of
alliance with more established enterprises. These three forces cannot
be understood in isolation. New firm creation requires venture capital, which is attracted to the opportunities created by the technologies

131

emerging from university research. Public equity markets provide liquidity (and rewards), which is what attracts the entrepreneurs and venture capitalists in the first place. And established enterprises provide both a source of funding for new ventures and access to product markets.

Together these forces comprise a system for monetizing intellectual property. Biotechnology became a business when the know-how emerging from scientific research became IP that was valued (in monetary terms) and bought and sold through various channels (markets). New firm formation is one of the ways that IP is monetized. Venture capitalists provide a mechanism to value IP and to fund its monetization; public equity investors provide the opportunity for liquidity; alliances provide means to value and trade IP. In this respect, biotechnology looks a lot like other sectors. Similar arrangements and forces are at work in software, semiconductors, information technology, and communications. This chapter asks how well these arrangements work in biotechnology, and specifically, how well they meet the functional requirements laid out in chapter 4: managing risk, integrating, and learning.

SPAWNING NEW FIRMS

Recall from chapter 5 that the biotechnology industry has been characterized by one wave of start-ups after another throughout its entire history. The well-known giants of biotech (Amgen, Genentech) aside, this sector is composed of relatively small and young firms. Where do they all come from, and why do we see so many?

There are essentially two sources of new biotechnology firms: academics who start or who participate in the founding of new firms, and scientists or managers who leave existing biotech or pharmaceutical firms to start their own firms. This distinction, in practice, however, can be blurry. Even firms founded by nonacademics generally include academics as part of scientific advisory boards or retain leading academic scientists as consultants. The prominent role of universities in the spawning of new biotech firms has been well documented.[1] New biotech firms tend to be located near major biomedical research universities and academic hospitals (e.g., Cambridge, the San Francisco Bay area).[2] A 2001 Ernst & Young survey found that one in four U.S. biotech companies was located within thirty-five miles of a University of California campus. One in three California biotech companies was founded by University of California scientists.[3] Kelley Porter, Kjersten Whittington, and Walter Powell collected data on the founders of fifty-two of fifty-seven biotech companies in the Boston area and found that 131 individuals were involved in creating biotech firms between 1980 and 1997. Fifty-two percent of them were faculty from a university, and nearly all of them retained an affiliation with their universities.[4]

If we look at equity holdings of both universities and faculty at biotechnology firms at the time of their IPOs, we see a similar pattern. An analysis by Mark Edwards of Recombinant Capital revealed that a university had an equity position in 41 percent of the biotechnology firms that did an IPO in 2004; a faculty member had an equity position in 50 percent of the biotech IPOs for that year. In 1997, 30 percent of the biotech IPOs included a university as an equity holder and 53 percent had a faculty member.[5]

Why has biotech continued to spawn new firms over such a long period? At first glance the answer seems obvious. Universities are doing the cutting-edge basic scientific research that creates the opportunities for new firm formation. Moreover, the passage of the Bayh-Dole Act encouraged universities to patent their IP and take steps to commercialize it. Rapid technological cycles and the universities' incentives to commercialize their technology are necessary but not sufficient explanations for new firm formation—as an alternative, universities could license technologies to existing firms.

Why are so many start-ups (both faculty-affiliated and not) created to commercialize new science? Posed differently, why does technology transfer so frequently occur through new firm formation rather than through a collaboration between the university and an existing firm? The first explanation has to do with potential demand from existing companies. In general, companies license-in technology that fits with their existing repertoire of technological capabilities and commercial interests. They look outside to fill specific needs or gaps in their portfolios. Because universities tend to be on the cutting edge of science, they are more likely to be working on things some-what outside the immediate needs of existing firms. What universi-ties have to offer (cutting-edge science) may not always be what existing firms demand (technology that fills a specific gap).

A second set of explanations is more institutional in nature. In order to license-in a technology, the would-be licensor has to know about the technology—it's hard to buy something you don't know exists! But in this regard the market for know-how is far from perfect. Information about what technology is available and the quality of that technology is highly asymmetric. Those closest to the research—the university scientists themselves—knew what was happening first-hand and had much better information about the scientific quality of the work. A pharmaceutical or biotechnology firm without a very close relationship to a specific university laboratory or even to a scien-tist in that laboratory might not even be aware of what technology has been discovered or what might be available for licensing. As the first to know about their discoveries, university scientists wishing to start their own firms clearly have an advantage in the process—*why* they would prefer to do so is discussed below. Venture capitalists often maintain close ties with university technology transfer offices and faculty at major research universities in order to keep tabs on oppor-tunities for starting a new firm.

Even where information was available, it is not at all clear that internal and external parties would compete on equal basis for the rights to intellectual property. For instance, Eli Lilly tried to acquire a license on a technique for recombinant insulin invented by renowned Harvard biologist Walter Gilbert but lost out to Biogen, a firm founded by Gilbert.[6] There is no systematic data available on deals that did not take place; thus it is hard to determine the number of cases where established companies tried but failed to secure IP from a university. Business development executives from pharmaceutical companies interviewed for this book, however, suggested that it would be ex-tremely difficult for an external company to secure rights to discover-ies generated in a university if the relevant faculty members were interested in securing the rights for companies with which they had an affiliation. The data presented earlier on the high incidence of equity holdings of both universities and faculty in IPOs suggests that there may be strong financial incentives for universities to license start-ups instead of established firms. Thus even where there is latent demand for university technology from existing firms, informational asymmetries and institutional barriers may limit realization of this demand.

In essence, university scientists and the venture capitalists tightly linked to the social network have an "inside edge" on acquiring the rights to commercialize university-generated science. Even when existing firms know about the technology and have a strong interest in licensing it, they face another disadvantage relative to a start-up. To get access to the relevant technological and scientific know-how (not just the IP, but the tacit knowledge as well), they need to recruit the scientists from academia or another firm that is deeply familiar with the technology. Herein lies a barrier to entry for existing companies. The newly formed firm can offer the scientist a highly leverage incentive—equity ownership—that is extremely difficult for incumbent firms to replicate. Going right back to the beginning of the industry, Genentech's spectacularly successful IPO in 1980 made it clear that the personal financial payoffs from joining such a venture could be huge.

In theory, an enterprise could offer the same leveraged incentives as the start-up, but in practice this is generally not feasible. Established companies have salary structures based on existing norms and intraorganizational political considerations. While significant pay disparities exist within organizations, there are limits to how big these differences can be in practice. Even small entrepreneurial companies, for similar reasons, have practical limits on how far they can go in offering equity-based compensation to new employees. There are political considerations (why does employee A get a bigger chunk of equity than employee B?) but also financial constraints due to the capital structure of the firm.

Thus it is generally not feasible for any established company—whether a global multinational or a one-year-old start-up—to offer the same degree of highly leveraged compensation that a biotech venture could offer. University scientists choosing to leave academia and join a company faced professional risks. Many felt that the decision was irreversible: joining a company would end their academic careers. A similar career risk is felt by people employed at another firm. Only the potential benefits of equity-based compensation would be enough to make such risks worthwhile.

The reasons for new firm formation in biotechnology are not that different from other sectors. In biotechnology, the advantages of newly formed firms in competing for new technology are pronounced. In general, the new firm offers the potential for the inventor to appropriate handsome returns from their expertise. Furthermore, the inventor has a bargaining advantage in acquiring the rights to the technology because it needs them to succeed. There are many instances where academics are happy to remain in academia and to see their technology licensed to an existing firm (in return for royalties or research funding). But when the entrepreneurial bug bites, they have a pretty clear path to starting their own firms, provided they can secure the funding. And that's where venture capital comes in. With the availability of venture capital and public equity investors in search of the next Amgen, every new idea gets it own firm.

VENTURE CAPITAL AND PUBLIC EQUITY

New firms need capital. This is true in all sectors. The ability of the biotech sector to spawn new firms at such a high rate reflects more than just a high rate of opportunity created by scientific advance, the preference of academics to become entrepreneurs instead of employees, or the propensity of universities to license to start-ups. These factors could all be present, but without a fertile capital environment, there would be no start-ups.

The biotechnology sector has followed a familiar pattern found in other industries: venture capital has fueled the formation of new firms. Figure 7-1 shows the aggregate amount of venture capital raised by biotechnology companies over the life of the industry. Venture capital needs to be understood as both a source of funding and a mode of corporate governance. Venture capitalists do not just provide money; their investment comes with close oversight. The venture capitalist exercises control through various mechanisms, including representation on the board of directors, covenants and contractual restrictions, incentive arrangements, and the staging of capital infusions.[7] These

FIGURE 7-1

Cumulative VC funding for the biotech sector, 1978–2004

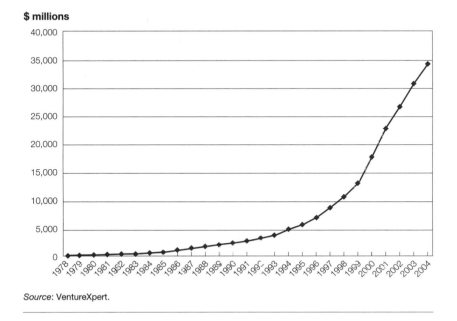

$ millions

Source: VentureXpert.

mechanisms are designed to alleviate one of the critical governance problems of new ventures asymmetric information. In general, the entrepreneur knows far more about the value of the opportunity than the investor. This information asymmetry potentially worsens as time unfolds. For example, the entrepreneurial team will be the first to learn of insurmountable technical problems in the product they are trying to develop. Venture capital can alleviate (but certainly not eliminate completely) the effects of these information asymmetries by providing various monitoring and control mechanisms.[8]

The other advantage of venture capital is that venture capitalists themselves become repositories for institutional knowledge about the industry. Typical venture capitalists see hundreds of business plans cross their desks. They invest in a large number of companies (as reported in figure 7-2 under number of deals). They have a window into the industry that few individual entrepreneurs have. And over

FIGURE 7-2

Number of deals, biotech firms, and VC companies

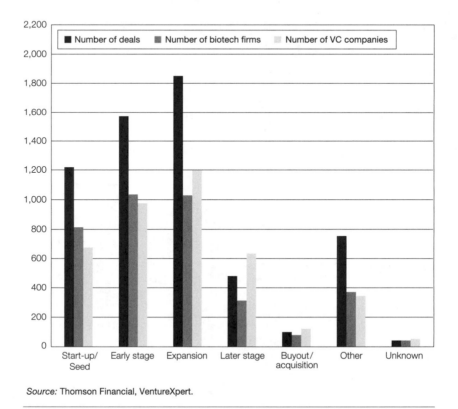

Source: Thomson Financial, VentureXpert.

time, they have accumulated experience as investors in hundreds of companies. They have seen most of the mistakes that can be made by a start-up team.

A great deal of research suggests that venture capital plays an absolutely critical role in stimulating innovation.[9] Indeed, outside the United States, where venture capital is less well developed, governments see the formation of a vibrant venture capital sector as one of the keys to stimulating innovation. In the context of biotechnology, there can be little doubt that venture capital has played a pivotal role in stimulating innovation through the formation of new ventures.

When it comes to biotech, however, there is a problem with venture capital. Venture capitalists typically have a time horizon of about three years. In addition, they invest in highly risky ventures. Thus they need to diversify their investments across a large portfolio of venture companies. As a result, even the largest funds cannot afford to sink a vast sum of capital into any one company. If we look at VC investments in biotech, we find that the average amount invested by a VC firm in a biotech company (all stages) is only $3.1 million. The maximum average amount given by a single VC firm to a biotech company is $20.2 million [10] Consider that it takes somewhere in the neighborhood of eight to twelve years for most companies to get their first drug on the market, assuming that they are lucky enough to succeed on their first drug. Chances are they will have a few failures along the way. During this decade-long journey, they will burn through $800 million to $1 billion. This is well beyond the scale of what venture capitalists can and will provide.

So how do biotechnology firms close the gap between VC and what they need? There are two sources. One is corporate partnerships and strategic alliances. We will discuss these below. The other is capital raised from public equity markets. Figure 7-3 shows the cumulative capital raised in IPOs and secondary offering of a comprehensive sample of biotechnology firms.

Figure 7-4 shows the annual investment sources by type. It is clear from the data that IPOs in biotechnology, like many other sectors, follow a cyclical pattern. The data also shows that public equity investors plays a very prominent role in the funding of biotechnology firms, even though most of those firms are at relatively early stages of commercial development when they go public.

Like venture capital, public equity needs to be understood as more than just a source of funding. It is also a governance structure. But the mechanisms of governance for public equity are quite different from those for venture capital. Because public equity markets offer investors liquidity, shareholders can exercise their exit option at almost any time. It is this exit option that offers shareholders of public companies their greatest leverage. If they think the prospects of the company have soured or the management is doing a poor job, they can sell their shares with just a few clicks of the keyboard. A liquid, well-functioning capital market is a powerful mechanism of corporate control.

However, a critical prerequisite for a public equity market to function well is rapid and uniform availability of information. Various

FIGURE 7-3

Cumulative proceeds from biotech equity issuances, 1978–2004

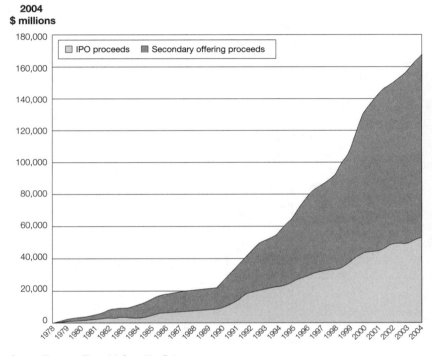

**2004
$ millions**

Source: Thomson Financial, Securities Data.

institutional arrangements and rules have evolved to facilitate information flow in well-developed capital markets. For instance, there
are disclosure rules that require companies to make public information that could have a material impact on the financial prospects of
the enterprise. There are accounting standards for how financial
information should be communicated and interpreted and for how
critical financial parameters should be measured. There are regulations that constrain when "insiders" can buy or sell stock. There are
also intermediaries, such as financial analysts and auditors, that play
a role in information dissemination. These intermediaries have at
their disposal various techniques, such as real option analysis and discounted cash flow, to estimate the value of the company.

FIGURE 7-4

Annual investment sources by type

**Amount invested
(2004 $ millions)**

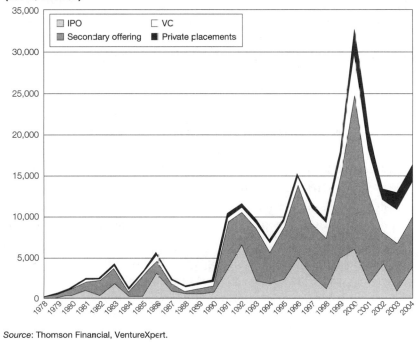

Source: Thomson Financial, VentureXpert.

We know from the accounting scandals of the past few years (e.g., Enron) that these mechanisms do not always work perfectly. Indeed, they can fail miserably. But in general they work relatively well for most types of businesses. Critical information, particularly about a company's financial prospects, is disclosed in a timely fashion and flows rapidly to investors and potential investors. This information drives the valuation of the company's stock. When information flows rapidly, we do not need the close governance of venture capital; we can let the market do the work for us.

In sum, public equity governance works best when the information needed to value the enterprises can be easily disclosed and analyzed through standard accounting and financial methodologies.

Private equity (venture capital) works best when we have highly asymmetric information that does not lend itself to standard accounting and financial evaluation. In those cases, we need tight governance and close monitoring. It is pointed out below that the characteristics of a typical biotech company are not well aligned with the properties of public equity governance; as a result, additional sources of funding and governance have been required. These additional sources of funding and governance have come from the emergence of a market for know-how.

MARKET FOR KNOW-HOW AND ALLIANCES

As discussed in chapter 5, Genentech's decision to enter a collaborative development and licensing agreement with Eli Lilly in 1979 was a watershed event. Genentech showed would-be entrants and, more importantly, venture capitalists, that intellectual property could be packaged and sold independently of the final product. IP was an asset that could be monetized. This was an incredibly important innovation for the industry. There was no way venture capitalists could provide the approximately $800 million in funding needed (and wait ten years) for a young biotech firm to get a drug on the market. And unless public equity markets were in a "bubble" cycle (as in 1999), it has generally been difficult for biotech firms to raise enough money from public offering to take their own drug all the way to market. How important have alliances been as a source of funding? Data compiled by Sean Nicholson and colleagues show that alliances contributed 45 percent of total financing raised by biotechnology firms in the 1990s.[11] In some years alliances constituted the single largest source of funding (e.g., in 1998 alliances accounted for 77 percent of financing of biotechnology firms).

The monetization of intellectual property required a market for know-how between biotech firms and more established enterprises. There are several reasons for the emergence of such an active market for know-how in biotechnology. First, biotech firms, as technology specialists, lacked the full complement of scientific, technical, and commercial skills needed to discover, develop, and market their own drugs. They needed access to these skills, and they found them in their more established pharmaceutical company partners. Second, as discussed earlier, pharmaceutical companies may have been at a disadvantage in licensing technology directly from universities, given informational and institutional barriers. As a result, if they wanted access to pursue leading-edge technology, they needed to go to biotechnology firms. From this perspective, the economic function of the biotechnology firm is to fill the gap between basic scientific research and early-stage drug discovery. Biotechnology firms are like middlemen in a R&D supply chain: they take on projects at early stages, develop them to some point, and then license (resell) them to pharmaceutical companies for further development.

A third reason has to do with overcoming one of the chief limits of public equity governance: information asymmetry. As noted above, venture capital investing, with its close monitoring and governance capabilities, was well aligned with the challenges of the relatively risky early-stage biotechnology R&D. Venture capitalists have visibility into the R&D process that public equity investors do not. However, it was also noted that the limits on the funding and time horizons of venture capital impel biotech to turn to public equity investors fairly early in their life cycles. For instance, in the period 1999–2001 only 25 percent of the biotech companies doing an IPO had any products in clinical development; the remainder were still in the preclinical and discovery phases of R&D.[12] By 2004 the figure had jumped to 88 percent, but still no companies had products on the market. Indeed, only approximately 20 percent of *all* publicly held biotechnology companies in existence today have any products on the market or are earning royalties based on products commercialized by partners. Thus the vast majority of publicly held biotech firms are essentially R&D entities.

Public equity was never designed to deal with the governance challenges of R&D entities. Consider the problem of valuation. Existing financial modeling methodologies are of little help: they rely on an analysis of historical earnings and earnings potential. Most biotech companies have no earnings (let alone an earnings history), and with their nearest products several years away and facing enormous technical and commercial uncertainty, it is hard to construct any reasonable valuation model. To value an R&D project, many questions need to be asked about the project itself having to do with the underlying technology and quality of the science, the molecule and how similar molecules have faired, the quality and experience of the team assigned to the project, the development plan (e.g., trial design), and the likely technical problems (e.g., potential manufacturing difficulties). Now consider the fact that R&D projects are engines of information creation. The best guesses at answers to all of these questions, and many more, are updated fairly regularly. It is not a one-shot deal.

Managers inside a company know this, and so they create internal mechanisms (e.g., R&D reviews, portfolio management committees) to keep themselves up-to-date. As anyone who has been involved in this process can attest, there is a real art of project selection and portfolio management. Rarely do you have all of the information you need to decide which projects to advance, which to kill, and which deserve more (or fewer) resources. In addition, the devil is in the details. A clinical study may come back with a strange anomaly (e.g., a very small number of patients experienced an unexpected side effect). It is actually hard to tell whether this is a big deal unless one really digs into the details of the study. Even then, experts might reasonably disagree.

For publicly held companies, there are detailed disclosure rules regarding financial information, detailed rules regarding how certain transactions should be accounted for and valued, and standards for valuing certain physical assets. However, when it comes to intangible assets in general, and R&D projects in particular, there are far fewer clear standards. Generally Accepted Accounting Principles (GAAP) generally do not require disclosure of R&D projects. Even in pharmaceuticals and biotechnology, where companies must disclose information on the state of their development pipelines, the level of detail in the disclosure varies significantly across companies and projects.[13] Companies have discretion, for instance, in how much detail they will provide about the therapeutic indications of the product under development, previous clinical trial results and progress, and future development plans.

The other challenge for investors is interpreting publicly announced trials results. Suppose a company announces that it has just completed Phase 1 clinical trials on a novel compound. Based on the results, it has decided to move the compound into Phase 2. Now suppose a different company developing a similar compound announces that after completing Phase 1 trials that it has decided to stop further development. Normally, we would think that the former company has good news and the latter has bad news. Indeed, the first firm's stock is likely to rise, and the second company's stock will probably fall (all things being equal). But is this evaluation justified?

Companies may set the bar very differently on drugs advancing from one stage to the next in clinical trials. Unless there are extreme results (e.g., the drug is proving toxic), much of the decision to advance a drug comes down a complex mixture of scientific and economic judgment. Specifically, it comes down to risk. The company that advanced its drug may have had fairly mediocre results but chose to continue development because it was willing to take more risks. Or it might have had fewer alternative prospects for development. For instance, it might not have had another drug to develop, so killing the Phase 1 project would have meant shutting down the company. The company might have been rewarded for advancing a project whose ultimate prospects are questionable. And the cost of killing the project later is obviously greater. The second company, which was probably punished by the capital markets for its "failure," might have done so because it set a higher standard for acceptable development risk. It might have had several other back-up compounds at early stages of development and thus felt more comfortable in killing a questionable project.

This is an interesting parable, but does this reflect reality? The available evidence suggests that it does. A 2004 study by Ilan Guedj and David Scharfstein of 235 cancer drug development projects revealed that firms of different sizes and with different financial resources make very different decisions about moving projects through early and intermediate stages of clinical trials.[14] They found that bigger firms tend to move projects forward from Phase 1 to Phase 2 at a higher rate than smaller firms. They also found that smaller firms (which presumably have a smaller number of alternative projects) with more cash move drugs from Phase 1 to Phase 2 at a much higher rate than firms with less cash; however, these same firms tend to experience a much higher rate of failure in Phase 2. The findings suggest that firms with cash tend to make poorer decisions (perhaps due to the inability of investors to closely monitor management) regarding the advancement of drugs in clinical trials.

One potentially critical role of alliances is to help address this information gap. If the general public investor is playing the role of the uninformed "tourist," the big pharmaceutical companies, with their years of experience and armies of scientists, are more akin to "locals" and surely have better knowledge about projects' technical and commercial prospects. Valuations of biotech firms tend to increase when they strike deals with larger, more established companies, indicating that some type of validation effect is at play. If Merck or Novartis or Eli Lilly were willing to invest in a biotechnology company's project, this was, in theory, a signal that the project's prospects were good. Moreover, while the public investor may not be able to monitor the risks of a development project and to make sure management is acting in the best interests of shareholders, a major corporate partner presumably can. I return to this point below.

EVALUATING THE SYSTEM OF IP
MONETIZATION

Together, the university-spawned firms, the funding mechanisms, and the market for know-how constitute a system for innovation through the monetization of IP. There is a certain compelling logic to this system. Universities initiate the science; highly motivated academic entrepreneurs with deep knowledge of the science carry that science into the commercial sector through the formation of new firms, aided first by venture capitalists and then by the public equity markets; finally, more established firms, with both capital and with competences in drug development and commercialization, collaborate with new entrants through the market for know-how to get drugs to patients. The parts seem to fit together quite well, and the system has some appealing properties. The earliest and riskiest phases of the process are put into the hands of entrepreneurs; strong incentives are at work; and there are economies of specialization as different types of organizations (universities, small firms, established firms) focus on different but complementary roles in the process. Indeed, the system appears similar to what has worked well in other sectors. But there are further questions to explore: Does it really work here? What are the properties of this system in terms of its ability to efficiently and effectively manage risks, achieve the requisite integration, and facilitate long-term learning? It is these issues that are addressed in the following sections.

Risk

Three properties are essential for any system for managing risk efficiently. The first is the ability to generate a broad diversity of options and experiments. It is hard to diversify risks with a limited number of bets on the table. The second is the ability to generate and diffuse relevant information. Risk is all about uncertainty, and uncertainty, by definition, is a lack of information. Managing risks is all about generating or acquiring and using the relevant information. You cannot make risk management decisions (e.g., whether to terminate an investment or continue investing) without a way of generating or acquiring the relevant information (e.g., whether or not a project is likely to succeed). And from a financial perspective, you cannot price risk without good, up-to-date information. Finally, you need mechanisms for those who bear risk to appropriate returns on their investment. You do not take risks unless you get amply rewarded. The bigger the risk, the more reward you need to step up to the table.

Along these lines, the system for innovation in biotechnology aligns reasonably well with the requirements for efficient risk management. First, the system clearly does a great job creating a broad diversity of options and experiments—the spawning of thousands of new firms testifies to this. The financial structures, venture capital and the public equity market provide means for investors to diversify their risks. Venture capitalists can make small, staged investments in a portfolio of companies; public biotech investors can likewise diversify their risks through holding a portfolio of companies. Moreover, a receptive public equity market has provided a means for both venture capitalists and scientific entrepreneurs to appropriate significant upside financial rewards.

The market for know-how provides further means for risk to be diversified at the firm level. A young biotech firm with limited financial resources can hedge its risks (at a cost) by bringing in a larger corporation as a development partner. The market for know-how also makes it possible to "syndicate" risks by selling the rights to different therapeutic applications of a given R&D program to different partners. This is commonly done in biotechnology, where the small innovative firm retains rights to more specialized therapeutic markets (requiring only a small sales force) and licenses rights to the same drug for larger markets where the big pharmaceutical company can leverage its sales force. From the point of view of the large company, a portfolio of R&D alliances with younger companies provides a mechanism to hedge technological risks.

Thus, in terms of generating a large diversity of experiments and rewarding entrepreneurs for taking risks, the current system would seem to work quite well. However, when it comes to the information flows needed for risk management, we should be a bit more circumspect. As noted above, one of the rationales for alliances is that they help redress the potential information asymmetry that exists between public investors and the management of biotechnology firms. The evidence on whether this logic actually works in practice is mixed. Big pharmaceutical companies often do make alliances precisely in those areas where they lack expertise; that's the reason for the alliance in the first place. Yet there are many examples where big pharmaceutical companies have spent lavishly on alliances with little to show in return and, conversely, where they walked away from licensing early-stage drugs that eventually became blockbusters. And even when alliances are struck, information does not always flow smoothly between the R&D partner and the corporate partner. Moreover, rigidities in the contractual structure may make it difficult for pharmaceutical companies to terminate alliance projects as quickly as they might like. Guedj found evidence that licensed-in projects tend to fail at later stages than internally originated projects (even taking into account the high overall failure rate of in-licensed projects).[15] Corporate partners are probably better informed—but not perfectly informed. Even as they acquire information, contractual rigidities may prevent them from acting quickly. Thus while alliances certainly help reduce the problem of information asymmetry, it would be naive to believe that the problem goes away completely.

There are already some signs that existing mechanisms for risk management are breaking down for the truly high-risk projects. In the post-genomics bubble period, there was a marked change in the strategies of start-ups and the preferences of venture capitalists. Rather than forming so-called molecule-to-market companies whose first product revenues could be ten to fifteen years away, entrepreneurs and venture capitalists began to look for lower risk, faster payback models, such as in-licensing existing projects and products from other companies. For example, in the latter part of 2003, twenty-three biotechnology companies filed with the SEC to go public. Of these, fourteen had in-licensed their lead product after it had already started human clinical testing; two others in-licensed drugs already on the market.[16] Rather than trying to discover new compounds, many new entrants are focusing on refining existing compounds or developing new formulations. Thus while the sector is generating broadly diverse experiments, they may represent lower-risk profiles than has traditionally been the case.

Integration

Integration involves both the exchange of information and the coordination of decision making and problem solving. There are two basic ways of achieving integration. One is to have firms own the requisite pieces of the puzzle and manage the process of integration through their internal systems and processes. The other is to have a network of independent specialists who integrate through markets (alliances, licensing, collaboration, etc.). Both modes can work quite well, depending on the circumstances. Traditional pharmaceuticals was cast largely in the mold of the first mode; biotechnology much closer to the second.

New firms are specialists by necessity. They simply do not have the resources to build capabilities across the full tool kit. The vast majority of new biotech firms were formed to exploit a very specific scientific finding or body of work initiated at a university. There is much to be said for the benefits that such focus brings. A small team of highly dedicated, highly motivated scientists, unencumbered by existing organizational strategy and processes, pursuing a singular focus would seem to be a fertile approach to breakthrough science. And it is. But this way of doing things also means that the team works in isolation from other scientists and organizations that bring complementary tools and capabilities to the table. Through the proliferation of new firms, the biotechnology industry has created an archipelago of hundreds of specialized expertise islands.

To achieve integration—to link these specialized islands to the complementary capabilities needed for drug development—the sector relies heavily on the market for know-how. Alliances allow specialized biotechnology firms to access downstream complementary assets (e.g., development, manufacturing, marketing, and distribution) needed to commercialize a drug. The market for know-how substitutes for organizational integration as a means of bringing together the requisite complementary assets and capabilities. This mode of integration—the use of IP monetization and the market for know-how—works very well in industries like software and semiconductors. There are, for instance, semiconductor firms that simply focus on creating and selling bits of IP that are designed into other chips (by other companies) and then manufactured by another company (usually a specialist foundry). In software and semiconductors, the market for know-how is the mechanism of integration.

It is useful to reflect on the conditions that enable a market for know-how to provide the requisite degree of integration among specialized firms in industries like software and semiconductors. First, it helps to have modular designs with clearly defined, codified interface standards. Modularity enables a big problem to be broken into a set of quasi-independent subproblems. With clearly defined interface standards between the subproblems, modularity reduces communication and coordination costs between organizations working on different pieces of the puzzle. Software and semiconductors tend to be highly modular. Thousands of individual Linux programmers scattered around the globe can contribute to the Linux operating system because of its modular structure. They do not need to communicate with one another; as long as they follow the well-documented Linux protocols and standards, their code will be compatible. In software, well defined, broadly accepted platforms (like the Microsoft operating system) provide a mechanism to integrate the efforts of a diverse group of specialists.

A second requirement is technology that can be communicated and transferred in codified form (e.g., blueprint, lines of code). Software is completely codified (although the expertise to develop software is not). Semiconductor designs that are now created almost completely via computer are also highly codified. Once technology can be codified in digital form, it can be transferred around the world at trivial cost and time. This allows developers from dispersed parts of the world to collaborate and to transact and transfer their intellectual property at relatively low cost.

Biotechnology is quite different from semiconductors and software. The pieces of the drug discovery puzzle are often not modular at all but constitute a set of interdependent problems (see chapters 3 and 4). Subtle interactions between a target, a molecule's structure and its physical properties, dosage form, the manufacturing process, the dose, and the patient population can profoundly influence the performance of a drug. It is generally difficult to lock down any one parameter of the drug's characteristics without at least exploring the implications for other parameters. The process remains iterative and messy. Moreover, there is really no equivalent of a standard platform (e.g., an operating system). It is impossible, for instance, to declare that any company wanting to collaborate with Novartis needs to develop drugs with XYZ physical properties. Each project is unique.

Further complicating integration across firm boundaries is the fact that biotechnology, despite the growing use of bioinformatics and computer-aided drug discovery, still contains a strongly tacit dimension. What is known about a target or a molecule or the behavior of a drug inside the body cannot be completely codified or reduced to precise rules (if X, then Y). Data from experiments are subject to a high degree of interpretation and differences of opinion. What constitutes a strong signal of potential efficacy for one researcher may give pause to another, based on idiosyncrasies in their training and experiences. Posed differently, despite the advances in science, there is still an "art" to drug discovery that relies on judgment, instinct, and experience. As a result, shared experience is likely to matter. Whereas a Linux programmer never really needs to meet, let alone talk to, other members of the Linux community, scientists involved in drug R&D benefit from collective experience, or "team learning."

One of the factors potentially impeding information flow in biotechnology is concern over intellectual property protection. A market for any commodity (real estate, intellectual property) requires well-defined, well-protected property rights. We would hesitate to buy homes if we were not assured of a clear title to the property—that's why we do title searches and buy title insurance. The importance of protection is particularly important when it comes to IP because once such property is exposed, you cannot take it back, unlike a physical commodity like real estate. Thus the very act of shopping your IP puts it at risk. In the context of an ongoing development project, new IP is created and proprietary information must be continually shared.

Strong intellectual property protection in software and semiconductors supports the market for know-how. There are patent disputes, of course, as there are everywhere. Even former partners have sued each other over alleged breaches of IP (e.g., Apple versus Microsoft). But a piece of software code, for instance, is a fairly distinct entity that can be protected by legal mechanisms, and cheating can be detected relatively easily. The same is true in most areas of semiconductors. But in biotechnology the IP regime is more complex and murky. It is often not clear ex ante what is patentable and what is not. In addition, any given piece of IP may have elements that are patentable and others that are not. Furthermore, the most valuable IP is often not the specific molecule, but the understanding, insight, and data about how that molecule behaves, what it can do, what its potential problems are, and how it might be developed. This type of knowledge is often much more difficult to patent, and yet it needs to be shared before and during the collaboration.

Murky intellectual property creates two possible problems for integration. The first is ex ante restriction in information flow; the second is ex post contractual disputes. The first problem, while hard to observe, is a pervasive aspect of most collaborations involving technology. Sensitivity over proprietary information impedes the sharing of information that might be vital to the success of the product. This sensitivity exists because of the real and lurking possibility of the second class of problems: an ex post contractual dispute between partners. These are visible and often quite costly to the parties involved. In biotechnology, there are many examples of former partners or collaborators suing each other over IP disputes. Indeed, Genentech and Lilly, whose original deal over recombinant insulin became a template in many ways for the industry, wound up in a legal dispute over the rights to human growth hormone. Amgen and Johnson & Johnson codeveloped EPO but wound up in a bitter legal battle over the division of marketing rights. Years later, when Amgen developed a new version of EPO—pegasolated EPO—the companies wound up in litigation again over whether PEG-EPO constituted a completely new product or simply an improvement to the original version (and thus subject to the original licensing agreement). Boston Scientific ended up in court with its onetime manufacturing partner, Medinol, after it set up its own manufacturing plant in Ireland to produce a stent that allegedly infringed on Medino's patents.[17] These are just a few highly visible examples, but they illustrate the realities of collaboration in a context where intellectual property boundaries are not well specified.

Thus while on paper it appears that the market for know-how creates many bridges across the specialized islands of expertise, a closer examination suggests otherwise. This is not software or electronics. The technology is not modular; it is not well codified; and intellectual property concerns often restrict critical information flows. True integration under these circumstances is extremely rare.

Learning

Learning, at an industry level, can occur through three channels. One is the Schumpeterian process of "creative destruction," in which new entrants bring new knowledge, skills, and technologies into the industry. The competitive process enables the superior techniques (and the firms that have them) to push aside the inferior ones. Examples from other settings of this process include new semiconductor firms replacing vacuum tube producers, personal computer manufacturers (like Dell) replacing minicomputer manufacturers (like DEC), and mini steel mills replacing integrated steel mills. The second channel is imitation. Firms can learn by imitating others. The third channel is learning from one's own experience.

All three can be at work at the same time in an industry, and indeed often complement one another. However, each channel tends to be suited to somewhat different types of knowledge and technologies. For instance, creative destruction tends to involve technologies and skills that are both radically different from existing capabilities and that can stand alone. In previous research, my collaborators and I found that relatively codified knowledge tends to be learned through imitation, but that relatively tacit knowledge has to be acquired through experience.[18] Thus the mode of learning in an industry matters because it influences the type of knowledge that tends to be developed.

Given the high rate of entry and new firm formation, biotechnology appears at first glance to be a classic case of Schumpeterian creative destruction: new entrants were the carriers of new waves of science, each of which brought expectations, at least from some observers, that the new entrants would displace incumbent pharmaceutical firms as the dominant players. However, with the exceptions of Genentech and Amgen, it is hard to argue that this vision has become a reality. Biotech firms have not displaced big pharma, despite the latter's struggles. This is not to say that new biotech firms have not been carriers of new knowledge, skills, and competences. They have been. But they have not been able to displace large pharmaceutical players, because biotechnology firms generally lacked all the critical downstream complementary capabilities (clinical trial expertise, regulatory knowledge, distribution) and financial resources to enter on their own.

Learning by imitation in biotech is stimulated in various ways. One is through the new firm formation process. Recall the evidence presented in chapter 5 that new entry in specific technologies tends to take place in waves—there was not just a handful of combinatorial chemistry firms; there were more than fifty. In part this is due to the diffusion of basic scientific knowledge through conferences and publications, but it is also due to the behavior of venture capitalists. Imitation is also stimulated by the public equity capital markets as investors' appetites for certain types of technologies ebbs and flows. And finally, the market for know-how almost certainly leads to some degree of imitation as firms shop their technologies and as they learn through their collaborations.

The same factors that stimulate learning through imitation may actually impede learning through experience at the firm level. The high rate of firm formation means that there are many inexperienced firms in the industry. The typical start-up in biotech is simply going to lack the capabilities of a Genentech, which has accumulated R&D experience for more than thirty years. In addition, because newer ventures have limited financial resources, they simply cannot afford to learn through experience. If they fail, they are finished. The pressure on biotech firms is to succeed the first time (if they do, and the hit is big enough, they will have enough cushion to learn). Diversified investors do not need to wait for any given biotech firm to perfect its craft. And given that venture capitalists are focused on a liquidity event in a three-year time frame, they have little incentive to promote learning at the organizational level. Finally, the market for know-how may also impede learning from experience. The average R&D alliance in biotechnology lasts less than four years (about one-third of the expected product development cycle). Alliance partners are interested in the firm achieving its next milestone, not in building long-term capabilities. If the biotech firm cannot achieve its milestones, the partners have an easy option to terminate the relationship.

There are exceptions. Established biotech firms, like Genentech, Amgen, Genzyme, and Biogen, and of course the major incumbent pharmaceutical firms have incentives to learn from their experiences, although they too face capital market pressures to perform and are penalized for failure, regardless of how much they learned. However, the bulk of the biotech industry is not organized to learn from experience. This means that much of the tacit technical and organizational knowledge needed to do R&D well is not accumulating in the industry. We should not be surprised that new firms are less productive, in many respects, than firms with years of experience. Nor should we be surprised that a sector that has continued to spawn new firms—the average age of firms in the sector has remained relatively constant over time—suffers from productivity problems. We essentially have a sector that has stayed—in aggregate—at the top of the learning curve.

CONCLUSION

The proliferation of new ventures, the availability of private and public equity funding, and the creation of a market for know-how constitute a powerful system for undertaking innovation. This system has worked remarkably well in other high-tech sectors. But the conditions that allow it to work well in those sectors—codified technology, modular designs and standard platforms, and well-delineated intellectual property—are often lacking in biotechnology. As a result of this system of innovation, the biotechnology sector has evolved an anatomy—small, specialized firms, integration by means of alliances, etc.—that, while doing certain things well (e.g., generating many experiments, encouraging risk taking, learning through imitation), falls short in other areas (integration, learning from experience). Chapters 8 and 9 consider the implications of the foregoing analysis in terms of strategies, business models, institutional arrangements, and policies.

PART III

THE SCIENCE-BASED
ENTERPRISE

8

Organizational Strategies
and Business Models

P revious chapters have essentially identified and diagnosed the problem: the scientific and commercial promise of biotechnology has been impeded by the way the business is structured and operated. Whereas the effective development and application of the technology requires integration, the business of biotech is driven by specialization and fragmentation; whereas the uncertainty and novelty of the science requires rapid diffusion of "high fidelity" information, the business strategies of biotech firms impede information flow; whereas the science requires long-term cumulative learning, the biotech firms face market pressure to optimize short-term perceptions of value. In part these problems have arisen due to exogenous, institutional conditions such as government policies, the functioning of capital markets, and regulations. However, the problems are also rooted in the behaviors and strategies of biotechnology and large pharmaceutical companies themselves. The final two chapters of this book explore, respectively, possible solutions from both the firm-level strategy perspective and the broader institutional environment perspective.

This chapter focuses on the strategies and business models biotech and established pharmaceutical companies might deploy to improve their performance. The imperfect and often messy context in which these firms operate is taken as a given, and it will not, for the purposes of the discussion here, be assumed to change dramatically over the foreseeable future. Investors will be fickle and sometimes irrational. Academic entrepreneurs will continue to be motivated to start their own firms, whether this strategy is rational or not. Venture capitalists will still feel impelled to take companies public at the earliest opportunity. Public equity markets will be what they are with all their strengths and limits. There are likely to be bubbles and, of course, busts as well. Whether any of these things are good, bad, inefficient, or efficient is moot: this is the world that modern companies, including biotechnology companies and big pharmaceutical companies, must navigate. But what strategies and institutional arrangements might be feasible and desirable if our goal is to both make the biotechnology sector economically healthy and make it realize its potential to transform health care?

Some Words of Caution. The focus of this chapter is practice. What should managers and firms be doing to improve performance? There are no easy answers, nor does anyone (including this author) have very good data to demonstrate which practices work better than others. These data are quite simply not available because biotechnology is too early in its life cycle to observe stable patterns of performance. If one studies, for instance, the automobile industry, the data show pretty consistently over a very long time that Toyota has evolved better development and manufacturing capabilities than many other auto companies. One can conclude with some confidence that Intel and Microsoft have been doing something right. Their performance in product development and profitability has been sustained over many product generations.

In contrast, for biotechnology, our ability to draw inferences from specific company examples is constrained by relatively short time frame, the highly stochastic nature of drug R&D, and the small sample of "winners." Drug development is a low-probability game with highly skewed returns to success. Amgen is clearly a very successful enterprise. Today it is the highest valued biotech company by market capitalization (and about fifth among all pharmaceutical companies in the world). Does this make Amgen's strategy the right one? While it's hard to argue with success, Amgen would be a very different entity today had EPO failed in the clinic or had the company not succeeded in a pivotal patent dispute with its rival, Genetics Institute, which lost the case and was acquired by Wyeth Pharmaceuticals. This is not to say that some companies are not more capable than others or have "better" strategies, but simply that given the low numbers and the highly stochastic nature of the competitive process, some short-term luck (good and bad) makes it hard, at this point, to identify true best practices from specific firm examples.

Even among successful biotech companies, there are important differences in strategy. Amgen has achieved success through the successful commercialization of a few blockbuster drugs; Genentech has focused on smaller markets (like targeted cancer therapeutics); Genzyme has focused on drugs for very rare diseases. Existing models provide clues—but not necessarily answers.

The remainder of this chapter is divided into three parts. The next section focuses on the key strategic issues facing younger biotechnology firms, specifically on questions of vertical integration and organizational boundaries. A discussion of similar issues follows, but from the point of view of larger, more established pharmaceutical companies. The final section addresses alliances and alternative organizational models.

BIOTECHNOLOGY FIRMS: STRATEGIC PRINCIPLES, BUSINESS MODELS, AND ORGANIZATIONAL BOUNDARIES

Since the purpose of this section is to provide some guidance about strategy, it makes sense to start with goals. What does success mean in biotechnology? Let's start by emphatically stating what it does *not* mean. Being a successful biotechnology firm clearly requires access to capital as a means to achieve ends, but raising capital should not be an end in itself. This would not be a controversial statement in many industries, but it seems to contradict a prevailing view in the biotechnology industry itself. At any biotech industry conference and in any of the major biotechnology news outlets, the state of the industry's health is strongly equated with capital raised. A "banner year" in biotech has come to mean a year in which financing is plenty and the IPO market is hot. Again, it is important to stress that financing is extraordinarily important for this industry. It is its lifeblood. Without capital, one cannot do *anything* in this industry. However, capital is an input, it is not an output. A venture capital round or an IPO or secondary offering are financing events. They are not a measure of performance, nor are they signs of success. They may be signs of how others perceive a firm's or the industry's *prospects* for future success, but they do not constitute success. Raising a lot of capital is a two-edged sword. It means some group of people (investors) thinks you have great prospects. Now you have to live up to those expectations. Raising capital in biotech is like getting an official number for the Boston Marathon. It can be really tough to do it, and you need to qualify, but it only gets you into the race. You still have to run the 26.2 miles!

A related misconception in the biotechnology concerns business development deals: alliances, licensing agreements, partnerships, etc. Alliances in biotechnology are an extremely important strategic tool. They are not, however, the endgame. Yet the IP monetization mind-set that grips the industry often obscures this point. Companies that do lots of deals are viewed as successful. As a percentage of the total workforce, biotech may have more people involved in business development than any other industry (almost certainly the highest per dollar of revenue). But, as in the case of financing, doing a deal signals *potential*; whether value will ultimately be created depends on the execution of the project. Deals alone can never create value. They can only (if properly structured) unlock value that exists and enable value capture. Deals and deal structure are extremely important to the success of individual firms and to the growth of the sector. But deals are a means, not an end. What matters is how effectively an organization or industry uses the capital its raises, and more specifically, how well it creates true value from its activities. Ultimately, value creation and capture are what matters.

Perhaps simply breaking the IP monetization mind-set around financing and deal making would help the sector perform better. However, excellent performance requires more than a change in mind-set. It requires the crafting and implementation of proper value-creating strategies. One of the fundamental strategic questions facing biotech (and major pharmaceutical companies) concerns vertical integration and organizational boundaries. For younger biotech companies, the question is generally focused around the extent to which the firm should vertically integrate downstream into later-stage development, manufacturing, and even marketing. In essence, this question gets right to the heart of the question: What is a biotech firm?

Vertical Integration and Organizational Boundaries

Think of the strategic problem facing a biotech firm that has developed a molecule it thinks can treat certain cancers. It has done preliminary laboratory studies but has not yet begun human clinical trials. Should it sell the technology (license it out) to another company, or should it continue investing in the project itself? And if the company continues development, should it plan on manufacturing and marketing the drug itself or find a partner? What type of relationship should it have with a partner or set of partners? On the surface, finance alone might be seen as the determining factor. Can it afford to develop the project itself? Can it afford to manufacture and market the drug itself? Indeed, the vertical integration strategies of many biotechnology companies have been driven by the availability of financing. When the market for biotech equity is good, and they can raise money, they try to vertically integrate; when things are tight, they look for partners. Clearly, the availability of financing operates as a huge constraint on what strategies smaller firms can pursue. However, it should not be the sole driver of the strategic choice. Just because a company can afford to do something, it does not mean that it should.

Vertical integration is sometimes justified on economic grounds, but sometimes it is not. Outside of biotech, there are many examples of companies that have done quite well by controlling upstream IP and licensing it (for handsome returns) to other companies. Microsoft, for example, has earned handsome profits by licensing its Windows operating system to computer companies rather than vertically integrating into computer hardware itself. "Star" book authors or entertainers follow a similar strategy. They earn significant returns on their intellectual property by licensing others (publishers, record companies, etc.) to publish and distribute their work. Authors like Stephen King or entertainers like Madonna do not need to own their own book companies or record companies to capture significant returns on their work. They, like Microsoft, are using the market for IP.

The opposite view holds that biotech firms should never vertically integrate but instead should "stick to their knitting"; that is, they should focus on their core competence of research and extract rents on their IP through licensing (much the same as Microsoft does). Proponents of this view tend to see vertical integration as an outdated model for organizing innovation. Instead, they envision networks of highly specialized firms (small firms doing research, big firms focused downstream) working together through the market for know-how.

The issue is more subtle than just choosing which strategy is best. Both vertical integration and licensing can be great strategies depending on the context and the conditions. In the case of biotech, the issue hinges on how well markets for know-how work. When markets for know-how are working well (as they tend to do, for example, in software) out-licensing strategies can be very effective and very lucrative for players with scarce and valued IP. They also promote innovation. When conditions exist that impair markets for know-how, vertical integration strategies are needed to overcome critical barriers to innovation. Of course, we need to keep in mind that the choice between vertical integration and out-licensing is really a continuum, with many intermediate forms of governance—such as alliances and long-term collaborative relationships.

When Markets for Know-How Fail

Research conducted over the past twenty years suggests four basic factors that need to be considered in determining whether or not a market for know-how will work: (1) the degree of *information asymmetry*, (2) the need for investments in *specialized assets*, (3) the *tacitness* of the know-how, and (4) the degree to which the relevant *intellectual property* can be protected legally.[1] Each of these is explained briefly below.

Information Asymmetry. Information asymmetry refers to the differences in information available to sellers (innovators) and buyers (would-be licensees). The bigger the differences, the harder it is to come to mutually agreeable terms on things such as value. Proprietary or tacit information can create barriers to information exchange. Information asymmetry helps to explain a fairly common and yet somewhat paradoxical phenomenon in biotechnology. Young biotechnology firms often complain that large pharmaceutical companies undervalue their technology, while the latter complain that they often pay too dearly for technology with poor prospects. Neither buyer nor seller is happy because their expectations are based on fundamentally different information. High information asymmetry creates a barrier to innovating through a market for know-how.

Specialized Assets. An asset that once created cannot be easily redeployed to an alternative valuable use is considered specialized. For instance, clinical data showing how a particular drug works is a very valuable asset to the company trying to market that drug, but it is probably worth very little to another company that does not have the rights to market the drug. Specialized assets create problems in markets because they create an effect known as lock-in. Once a party makes investments in specialized assets, the costs of getting out of that relationship increase This leads to serious attenuation of ex post bargaining power. The need to make highly specialized investments creates a barrier to innovation through the market for know-how.

Tacitness. Tacit knowledge is knowledge not fully articulated or describable by the people who possess it. Organizations, like individuals, can possess tacit knowledge. Organizational skills and capabilities based on tacit knowledge are not perfectly repeatable and are extremely difficult to transfer across organizational boundaries. Even if it wanted to, BMW could probably not transfer its design skills and capabilities to another organization because many of those skills are tacit. Tacit knowledge is difficult to transfer.[2] It thus increases the costs of collaborating in markets for know-how and impedes innovation through interfirm relationships.

Intellectual Property Protection. Property rights enable markets to work. No one will buy what they cannot be secure in owning. When knowledge cannot be protected legally, it is difficult to transact. The buyer is clearly taking a risk, but the seller can as well. Transacting know-how exposes it to imitation without compensation (in spite of secrecy agreements). In addition, when the boundaries of the know-how in question are not clear, the process becomes enormously complex. The seller may have expectations that they are selling one thing (of narrow scope) and the buyer has expectations of buying something else (usually broader in scope). Weak IP protection impedes innovation through the market for know-how.

Implications and Applications
for Biotech Firm Strategy

These four factors can help us understand when markets for know-how are likely to work, and thus where IP monetization through licensing is likely to be viable, and, conversely, when companies should vertically integrate. In the context of biotechnology and pharmaceuticals, we have a broad range of technologies and projects that span the spectrum of these four factors. This suggests that different business models may be viable and appropriate for different kinds of technological innovation. In biotechnology, there have been essentially four broad classes of technological innovation: (1) novel research methods and tools (e.g., high throughput screening, combinatorial chemistry, genomics, structure-based drug design); (2) identification of novel mechanisms of action or targets (e.g., angiogenesis, RNAi); (3) creation of novel compound types (rDNA, MAbs); and (4) development of novel treatment modalities and therapeutic markets (e.g., gene therapy, personalized cancer vaccines, drugs for rare genetic diseases). There is broad variation even within these categories, so we need to be cautious in our interpretations. Nevertheless, based on this framework, there appear to be some very different business models across class of innovation.

Novel Research Methods and Tools. As described in chapter 2, a significant share of biotechnology innovation has concerned the development of new methods, tools, and processes for identifying potential drugs or probing the molecular underpinnings of disease (identification of targets). Within this category we can include such technologies as high throughput screening, combinatorial chemistry, structure-based drug design, genomics, bioinformatics, and systems biology. Let's consider the alternative business models for a company trying to commercialize innovations of this type. One strategy would be simply to license the *use* of the technique to drug companies that would use it in their own discovery process. A second strategy would be to use the technology but sell drug discovery services based on the output of the tool (e.g., molecules, gene targets, information, "hits," etc.). A third strategy would be to vertically integrate forward into drug R&D and commercialization, that is, use the tool to discover and develop proprietary molecules.

Our framework identifies the potential issues and risks associated with the first strategy. First, to the extent the technique is highly novel, it might be difficult to convince potential licensees of its value (asymmetric information). Virtually all new research methods in the life sciences have been greeted initially with skepticism. It is hard to validate or verify the value of a technique without actually using it. Second, application of the technique is likely to require investments in specialized knowledge or equipment. Such investments raise the risks to licensees because they are not redeployable to alternative uses. Third, while many aspects of new research techniques can be described in writing, there is often an element of "practice art" or experience required to become fully competent. The stronger the tacit knowledge dimension of the technique, the more difficult it will be to transfer it to would-be licensees. And of course a licensee that cannot master the technique will not ascribe the same value to it as the innovator. Finally, there is a risk to the innovator if the intellectual property surrounding the new technique is not "airtight." Marketing the innovation to potential licensees means explaining it in some detail, and therefore exposing it to imitation.

The second model is a service or tool company model. Under this model, the company sells services based on the use of the technique or sells tools, systems, instruments, or software, that embed the technology. Under this model, there is less need to convince potential licensees of the value of the technology prior to use. The innovator assumes the full risk of the value of the technology. If it turns out to be as productive as promised, the innovator can capture value on fees from the service or revenues from the tools. The pure service model has an advantage over the tool model. Customers of a service do not have to make technique-specific investments. Think about a firm buying combinatorial chemistry services. It is, in essence, purchasing molecules. These are really no different from what the firm is generating internally and thus it already has the infrastructure in place to handle them. The same is likely true of other techniques, such as genomics. The output from such techniques (molecules, targets, information) can be absorbed by drug companies without the need to make specialized investments. Likewise, the details of the technique are no longer an issue for customers in the service model. They do not need to learn to use the technique, but just consume the output. Finally, because the intellectual property stays within the innovator's boundaries, the risks of unintended spillovers and imitation are greatly diminished in this model.

The service model was followed by many "platform" technology companies in the late 1990s during the genomics boom. Yet many of the companies pursuing platform service models (Millennium, Celera, Human Genome Sciences, Incyte, etc.) abandoned this strategy and decided to vertically integrate downstream into the development of proprietary molecules. The framework above would call into question the rationale for such a strategy. Does vertical integration overcome problems of asymmetric information about the value of the technique? Potentially, yes, if quality of the technique's output is questionable: Are the targets valid? Are these promising molecules? Is this information valuable? However, it is unlikely that vertical integration is necessary to solve the other issues: specialized asset, tacit knowledge, weak intellectual property protection. The service or tool product company model is probably enough to deal with those issues. Thus vertical integration based on a platform technology or technique is likely overkill. Indeed, it may be a suboptimal strategy, considering that the firm probably lacks experience and capabilities in the relevant downstream activities needed to develop drugs (toxicology, formulation, regulatory, etc.).

Note, however, that being in the service or tool business offers a very different risk reward profile than being in pharmaceuticals. A company can be a very profitable following the service or tool model (e.g., Affymetrix), but it is not likely to be earn the enormous returns of a company that successfully develops drugs. The problem that many platform companies may have faced in the late 1990s was not with their models, but with the fact that the genomic bubble created unrealistic valuations that could not be sustained with a service or tool model.

Novel Targets or Mechanisms. Another major class of innovation in biotechnology concerns the identification of new disease targets or mechanisms of action implicated in specific diseases. Research on the potential role of angiogenesis in cancer is an example of this type of advance. There are many others, as the Human Genome Project uncovered vast new gene families and associated protein targets that are suspected of playing a role in a variety of diseases. There are many small biotechnology companies that have specialized in particular targets or disease mechanisms (e.g., EntreMed focused on angiogenesis). What is the right business model for such firms?

The framework highlights a few key issues. First, it is very unlikely that intellectual property can be completely secured on a mechanism or even an entire class of targets. Very often the research leading up to the target discovery is published and in the public domain. So IP in this space has more to do with scientific expertise and knowledge of how the mechanism works and its nuances. This immediately creates an information asymmetry problem, and may well create a problem related to the transfer of tacit knowledge. Therefore it is unlikely that a firm specializing in a novel mechanism or target can simply license its knowledge to another firm; rather, it may need to use this knowledge to discover and develop a drug. The

question then becomes whether it is necessary for the firm to vertically integrate all the way downstream into clinical development,
manufacturing, and marketing of the drug. This depends partly on the
characteristics of the drug and the market. If it is a chemically synthesized drug for a well-established therapeutic market (e.g., cholesterol
reduction, hypertension, diabetes), the rationale for full vertical integration is weak. Here, established players would presumably already
have in place the expertise and downstream assets needed to develop
and commercialize the drug. They would not encounter the risks of
investing in specialized assets. And if they have expertise, their information asymmetry advantages are lower. At the same time, the innovator is protected if it can garner IP protection on the molecule.

Tacit knowledge may be an issue if deep knowledge of the mechanism of action is needed to design the appropriate clinical trials and
if information generated from clinical trials likewise deepens knowledge of the underlying biology. This suggests a need for a tighter,
longer-term collaboration rather than a simple arm's-length licensing
or development agreement. Such collaboration allows both the innovator and developer to learn over time about the mechanism, the
underlying biology, appropriate molecular targets, and the clinical
design. Without a long term commitment, however, it is unlikely that
either party would be willing to share the relevant knowledge. Is full-
blown vertical integration required? Perhaps, but a more efficient
solution may again be to craft a long-term collaborative relationship
that provides both parties with incentive to share knowledge without
risks of being abandoned.

Novel Compound Types/Treatment Modality/Markets. A
third class of innovation in biotechnology has involved the invention
of new classes of therapeutic compounds (e.g., rDNA, MAbs, stem
cells), new treatment modalities (patient-specific vaccines, tissue
engineering), and the development of completely new therapeutic
markets (e.g., rare genetic diseases, personalized medicine). Like the
other categories of innovation discussed above, these types of innovations also involve potential information asymmetry and tacit knowledge. But because they also typically require significant investments

in specialized downstream assets (development, manufacturing, distribution), they raise strategic risks that are largely absent from the other classes of innovations.

Consider the case of rDNA and why a full vertical integration strategy may have been the most reasonable approach for commercializing that technology. (The same conditions applied in MAbs and in other novel treatment modalities, like personalized vaccines.) In the early 1980s rDNA was a radically new technology. The first-generation biotechnology companies formed out of academia had a deep understanding of the technology, which established pharmaceutical companies lacked. This immediately created an information asymmetry. How valuable was the new approach to drugs? Recall that there were many skeptics, particularly among the scientific ranks of most established pharmaceutical companies that were deeply steeped in the tradition of medicinal chemistry. In addition, rDNA required investments in specialized manufacturing facilities to facilitate fermentation or cell culture processes, which are vastly different from synthetic chemical manufacturing. And because rDNA processes tend to be highly specific to the product, such investments were not just technology-specific, but project-specific as well.

The novelty of rDNA created two other issues. The technology remained more art than science in the earliest days. There were not good analytical techniques to even characterize the big protein molecules created by rDNA methods. This was particularly true in the context of process R&D. As a result, there was a strong tacit dimension of rDNA technology. Transfer of rDNA-derived molecules from one partner to another was fraught with challenges. Finally, the intellectual property issues were far from clear. Could genetically engineered microorganisms be patented? Could naturally occurring proteins derived from rDNA be patented? Could all the variants of a given protein be patented, or just the specific version that was cloned? These were some of the questions facing the biotechnology pioneers. Figuring out the answers meant exposing IP to potential and actual collaborators without strong IP protection.

None of these impediments prevented collaboration. In fact, there was plenty of collaboration, as noted in chapter 5. But collaboration was, in some sense, a second-best strategy. It entailed risks, not only for the biotech firms that were selling technology, but also for major pharmaceuticals on the buy side of the market. Disputes among collaborators were not uncommon, perhaps the most visible being the dispute between Amgen and J & J over the allocation of EPO marketing rights and ownership of intellectual property. The framework also helps us to understand why a company like Eli Lilly was a first mover in biotech collaborations. In essence, its transactional risks of collaboration were lower due to the fact that it had years of experience in biologics production (porcine-derived insulin and naturally cultured human growth hormone) and already possessed many of the requisite downstream manufacturing and clinical development expertise. And because insulin already had an existing market, it involved lower technical and commercial risks. It is interesting to note that once biotechnology firms began to invest in rDNA products for novel therapeutic categories, established pharmaceutical companies played a less prominent role in commercialization of these drugs.

Vertical integration may reduce the risks of operating in an incomplete and inefficient market for know-how, but it raises other risks. Given the investments required to fund downstream assets (like manufacturing plants, etc.), it is more difficult to pursue a diversified R&D portfolio strategy. Indeed, younger firms pursuing the FIPCO model are forced into an all-or-nothing strategy. If their first attempt to bring a drug to market on their own succeeds, they can do quite well (Genentech); but, if it fails, they can find themselves in a disastrous situation with a dry drug pipeline (Cetus). Obviously, given the low probabilities of success of drug R&D, the latter would seem to be a more likely outcome than the former, unless a firm can afford to pursue enough R&D projects to hedge their risks. And this is unlikely unless the firm is blessed with a very generous capital market, or if the firm already has an existing stream of cash flow. Paradoxically, if the rationale for vertical integration is associated in general with technological novelty, then it may well be that existing firms that are already vertically integrated or that have a strong cash flow stream (from licensing) are much better positioned than start-ups to pursue the most novel technologies.

IMPLICATIONS FOR ESTABLISHED
PHARMACEUTICAL COMPANIES

Much of this book has focused on the trials and challenges facing biotech firms. However, as noted at the outset, the established pharmaceutical sector (including companies such as Pfizer, Glaxo, Merck, Novartis, Lilly, etc.) is clearly part of the biotechnology world and faces its own challenges. For most of the postwar era, the pharmaceutical industry has been consistently the most profitable sector of the U.S. economy by virtually any performance measure (return on equity, return on sales, etc.). This superior performance was based on four structural pillars: (1) latitude to charge relatively high prices, (2) long product life cycles, (3) "blockbuster" drugs, and (4) relatively high R&D productivity. These pillars have eroded significantly during the past decade and are likely to continue to do so in coming years.

Historically, pharmaceutical firms enjoyed an environment (in the United States) where a combination of a fragmented buyers and low political pressure enabled a high degree of pricing latitude. This began to change in the 1980s with the growth of managed care organizations that included pharmacy benefits as part of health insurance. In addition, as drugs pricing moved toward the center of the political stage, the pharmaceutical industry came under increasing pressures. The new Medicare pharmacy benefits law will only likely increase these pressures as the cost of providing drugs to senior citizens becomes a significant fiscal issue. And it is not just government policy that lurks in the shadows. Larger private corporations like General Motors that are suffering financially under the weight of their employee (and retiree) health benefits programs are actively looking for ways to reduce their pharmaceuticals costs. Pressure from private-sector companies may turn out to be even greater (and potentially more effective) than government pressures. As a record number of drugs come off patent in the next several years, the potential for achieving major price concessions will increase dramatically.

Pharmaceutical companies also historically enjoyed long product life cycles. Once novel drugs were launched, innovators generally had the market to themselves for many years, sometimes more than a decade. A combination of strong patent protection and limited diffusion of basic knowledge created strong protective barriers. Now, basic knowledge diffuses almost instantly around the globe. Few companies can dominate the science in a given therapeutic area. The scientifically and commercially "hot" areas (e.g., cancer, diabetes, obesity, depression) draw swarms of competitors. Any given product category can have dozens of competing products in development. Because many of these are different technologies, or different versions of the same technologies, no one player is likely to create a patent-based barrier to entry. As a result, periods of exclusivity can be extremely short. Even worse, a newly launched drug is vulnerable to being made therapeutically obsolete by another new drug long before its patent has expired.

Blockbuster drugs (many of which have become household names) have driven growth in pharmaceuticals. It costs about the same to develop and commercialize a drug with $500 million in sales as it does for a drug with $5 billion in sales. The economics are pretty straightforward. As companies become bigger, they need more blockbusters to maintain their growth trajectories. A company with $1 billion in annual sales only needs $100 million in incremental revenue to have a 10 percent growth rate. A company with $20 billion in sales needs $2 billion in incremental revenue. There is only one problem. There are predictions that blockbusters will get rarer as genomics and other technologies enable drugs to be more finely tailored to specific subpopulations of patients. The potential exists for that $5 billion drug to become fragmented into ten $500 million submarkets.

Finally, as discussed earlier, the pharmaceutical industry faces all the above issues at a time when its R&D productivity is at best stagnant—and probably declining. R&D productivity is the key to growth in pharmaceuticals, and improvements in this area will become even more critical as the industry confronts the threefold threat of price pressures, short product life cycles, and more fragmented markets.

A Biotech Strategy for Big Pharma

Over the past decade, big pharmaceutical companies have been searching for strategies to combat the above pressures. A number of companies could not resist the urge to merge. Mergers in the pharmaceutical industry are a puzzling phenomenon. Analysts generally cheer them; whenever a company is in trouble (due to pipeline issues), they usually clamor for a merger or acquisition. Yet on average, the track record for mergers and acquisitions (M&A) in terms of creating long-term shareholder value in pharmaceuticals appears to be exceedingly poor.

The logic behind M&A in pharmaceuticals is highly suspect. As a consolidation strategy, M&A is warranted in industries suffering excess capacity (e.g., steel, electronic components, commodity chemicals). Through M&A capacity can be wrought out of the industry and prices can be stabilized. There may be some excess capacity in pharmaceuticals, but that is not the industry's main problem. In pharmaceuticals, M&A may lead to onetime gains in eliminating redundancies (e.g., plants, sales forces, duplicate R&D operations), but once those savings have been made, there is still a growth problem to be solved. Furthermore, being twice as big sounds great, but it also means you have to grow twice as quickly in gross terms just to keep up. And there is little evidence that larger scale (beyond a point) in pharmaceuticals helps R&D productivity. Doubling the size of the R&D operation through a merger is only economically justified if the output of new drugs more than doubles. To date, the record on the effect of pharmaceutical M&A on R&D productivity is simply not that good.

So where does this leave big pharmaceutical companies? It is popular in some circles to argue that big pharmaceutical companies are "dinosaurs" with no future, or that their future lies in focusing on marketing rather than R&D. Both lines of thinking miss the enormous opportunity now before large pharmaceutical companies. Recall that one of the big challenges facing biotech is integration, the value of which lies in bringing together the right set of people and pieces to develop novel drugs. Integration requires some degree of scale—enormous scale is not necessary, but at the same time a firm cannot be too small. Structurally, even medium-sized pharmaceutical companies are well positioned to exploit the opportunities to assemble the pieces of the puzzle. Achieving this integration, however, requires an appropriate set of R&D capabilities and strategies. Organizational boundary issues are as important for major pharmaceutical companies as they are for smaller biotech firms.

Organizational Boundary Issues and R&D
Strategy for Major Pharmaceutical Companies

Established pharmaceutical companies live on the buy side of the market for know-how and thus face the flipside of the issues facing biotech firms. What kinds of R&D should they do in-house, and what should they acquire through alliances, development agreements, and licenses from outside parties? Some industry observers, and even executives within the industry, have expressed the view that established pharmaceutical companies should focus on sales and marketing, allowing smaller, more innovative biotechnology firms to develop products. This is akin to the movie business. Movie studios generally do not invent their own content. Independent producers and scriptwriters generally develop the movie concept and pitch that to the studio. This is analogous to a biotech firm's initiating a research project and seeking collaboration (licensing) with a major pharmaceutical partner.

To see whether the "movie studio" model would be appropriate for major pharmaceutical companies, it is useful to consider further what makes the model work in the movie business. If we subject the movie business to our markets for know-how framework, we see that it is well suited to this type of structure. Consider a script for sale. There is virtually no information asymmetry. Studios can read the script and learn what they need to about the story. Scripts are also available from a broad range of independent writers; the studio does not need to worry about becoming locked in to a single writer. By definition, a script contains little tacit information. It is completely codified. Finally, copyrights provide clear protection. The boundaries of the IP are unambiguous; what's in the script is clear.

This is not to say there are never disputes over scripts or problems in movie production. But it does draw attention to the fact that if we think about the movie business as a "model" for biotech and pharmaceuticals, we need to be careful. The "technology" of the movie business fits perfectly within our framework as a model that would support a very efficient and effective market for know-how.

One form of the movie studio model in pharmaceuticals could involve procuring rights to drugs after Phase 2-A or 2-B (in essence, after proof of concept has been established) and then focusing internal development of large-scale Phase 3 trials, regulatory approval, and distribution and marketing. Such a model is likely to work best for less scientifically or technologically novel drugs (existing targets, existing compound classes, existing treatment modalities and markets), for which the results of Phase 2 provide a relatively clear signal about the value and prospects of the drug. Less novel drugs entail the lowest challenges of information asymmetry; given their lack of novelty, presumably knowledge about what works and what does not is well diffused. Second, less novel drugs tend not to require new investments in specialized downstream assets. Thus the firm can leverage its existing clinical development, marketing, and distribution infrastructure (e.g., a large sales force dedicated to primary care physicians). And presumably these are classes of drugs for which the intellectual property protection is relatively well defined and easy to assess (comparison to other molecules can be made).

From a commercial perspective, there is nothing wrong with this model. It could be very profitable, particularly if a firm has the strong sales and marketing capabilities needed to differentiate the product in the market (through advertising, for instance). However, it is not an appropriate model for more scientifically or technological innovative types of drugs. Without strong internal scientific capabilities, it is virtually impossible to sort out which prospective projects are attractive and which are "lemons.' A certain degree of internal capability is required just to make the right deals. In addition, as discussed above, if we think about novelty in terms of the compound type, the treatment modality, or the market segment, there are a number of strategic risks of outsourcing development. The market for know-how becomes less efficient due to problems with information asymmetry, specialized assets, tacit knowledge, and intellectual property uncertainty. This leads to a somewhat counterintuitive conclusion (at least in terms of conventional wisdom): the advantage of vertical integration is that it circumvents problems of information asymmetry, specialized assets, tacit knowledge, and IP uncertainty. These are most likely to be the characteristics of more novel R&D efforts. Thus while conventional wisdom holds that alliance and R&D outsourcing are critical for innovation, vertical integration may actually be better suited to the most novel types of innovation.

Different kinds of innovation in the drugs create different kinds of strategic risks. Thus it is highly unlikely that we would have any one universally better organizational model for innovation by major pharmaceutical companies (movie studio model versus traditional fully vertically integrated). Presumably, we might see various business models corresponding to different technology strategy. Movie studio models will be pursued by firms focusing on sales and marketing of less innovative drugs; the market for know-how works quite well for these types of products. Vertical integration models will be pursued by those firms focusing on the most innovative, scientifically novel drug types. Given the breadth of technologies, it is likely that most firms will have to pursue a mixture of arrangements contingent on the technology: the most innovative drugs being developed through vertical integration, the least innovative drugs being "procured" on the market for know-how, and drugs of moderate novelty and complexity being accessed through longer-term alliances with selected partners.

Far from being dead, vertical integration has an important role to play in the future pharmaceutical industry. However, it is not a panacea. Organizations must develop the specific internal capabilities needed to integrate the complex pieces of the drug R&D puzzle. It does no good to be a vertically integrated enterprise and yet operate each major function or technical specialty as its own island of expertise. This merely duplicates many of the problems in the market for know-how without securing any of the advantages of the independent and highly motivated entrepreneurial firm.

IMPLICATIONS FOR ALLIANCES

The argument for vertical integration does not imply that alliances go away. Indeed, as noted above, alliances and partnerships will be a critical complement to internal R&D. In addition, alliances will help address one of the key challenges of vertical integration: creating incentive for experimenting with risky technologies. Given the breadth and rate of technological change, it will be impossible for even the largest companies to explore all the variations of the landscape. They will need to form relationships with outside parties (universities and biotechnology firms). And in some cases vertical integration is simply not feasible for an organization. The biotech firm may lack both the capital and the capabilities to move downstream. A big pharmaceutical company may be unable to attract the talent it needs, or it may lack the time to develop the requisite scientific and technological capabilities.

Thus collaborative modes of development will continue to play a role in the industry. However, the kinds of collaboration discussed here are quite different from the kinds of relationships currently seen in the biotech sector. To achieve the requisite integration and learning, alliances need to provide a credible long-term commitment; there must be open flows of information; governance must be flexible enough to enable adaptation to changing circumstances; both parties must learn from each other

Unfortunately, too often in biotech and pharmaceuticals, the terms "alliance" or "collaboration" are misnomers. It looks good on the press release and in the annual report to talk about one's "partners" and "collaborators." Virtually every company will call itself the "partner of choice" in pitching itself to potential collaborators. But looking beneath the surface of current relationships in biotech and pharmaceuticals, we find that most alliances are fairly arm's-length relationships. The typical contract duration for a biotech "alliance" is slightly less than four years.[3] This may sound long, but consider it is relatively short compared to the typical product development cycle, which may be three times that long. The relationship governance is often centered around meeting fairly specific (and short-term) milestones. Miss a milestone, and the alliance can be terminated. Both partners focus on holding each other's feet to the fire. The focus is too often on the deal, not on creating a long-term, value-creating relationship.

There is nothing wrong with project management rigor, of course. However, in a collaborative relationship, partners need to strike a balance. The incentive to invest in specialized assets, to share proprietary information, to learn jointly, and to take risks is seriously attenuated by the fear that the relationship can be terminated at a moment's notice. Collaborations require commitments beyond a single project or beyond the next milestone. Consider what would happen if inside a company an entire drug development team was fired for missing a milestone on a very complex and uncertain project. Fairly soon it would be hard to attract good people to the organization. And, realizing that the organization was not committed to them, people doing development would be on the constant lookout for new opportunities. Sharing information or contributing to other projects would likely be a low priority. If this does not look like a very attractive way to run an internal development program, then it is certainly not a very attractive way to run a development program with an outside partner.

True alliances also require an intensive degree of management (not lawyer) attention. Most organizations underestimate the amount of internal resources required to properly manage a collaboration. In fact, it is likely that collaboration requires *more*, not less, management attention and effort than internal projects. Internally, there are existing organizational routines (standard processes, norms, and procedures about how to operate). Quite a lot happens and many decisions get made on autopilot. With collaboration, these routines do not exist at the outset. Almost everything is an exception that needs to be managed and discussed. Thus collaborations are initially more cumbersome, slower, and less efficient than internal organization. Only through shared experience between two specific collaborators are the relevant organizational routines established. But this takes time, effort, and investment.

Today many companies focus on the number of alliances. Indeed, business development personnel are often rewarded based on the number of deals they can do. Companies love to report how many alliances they have—again, the monetization mentality at work. But quantity does not matter unless one is pursuing a movie producer model of pharmaceuticals. For more scientifically or technological novel projects, it is more effective to have fewer, deeper collaborations than many, shallow links. Instead of signing forty deals in one year, a pharmaceutical company may be better off forming a handful (five or six) long-term (five- to ten-year) relationships with a very select number of outside partners.

Such an approach suggests a very different contractual and governance structure than we currently see. For starters, it means defining relationships fairly broadly. Instead of a license for molecule XYZ, we might see collaborative relationships around specific therapeutic areas or target families. There would be true joint decision making around development issues. At the same time, both parties would have to be willing to give up control over decisions they often covet. In many alliances, the bigger (more powerful) partner often seeks to retain as much control as possible under the assumption that they know best. For firms following a model of fewer but deeper alliances, partnerships are not formed unless both partners have confidence in each other's capabilities: if you are not willing to cede some control, you probably have the wrong partner. In all likelihood this means that far fewer firms will be desirable partners.

CONCLUSION

This chapter examines the various structural business models that both biotech and established pharmaceutical companies might pursue. The discussion suggests that a healthy anatomy of the biotech and drug sector includes a variety of business models, each targeted to different categories of innovation. Solving the structural issues, however, is only one dimension of the problem of making biotechnology a science-based business. Biotechnology operates within a context of other institutional arrangements (funding, universities, etc.) that exert pressures on firms to act in certain ways. In addition, managing the science-based enterprise involves challenges that stretch our current management technologies as practiced in other industry contexts. The final chapter explores what institutional changes may be required to support economically healthy science-based enterprises.

9

The Path Ahead

Scientific revolutions like biotechnology are only partly about science. Inextricably linked to the science are experiments in institutional arrangements, organizational forms, business models, and management practices. Technological innovation and organizational and institutional innovation are often so tightly intertwined that it makes little sense to discuss what came first. Did the technology trigger the need for organizational innovation? Or did the organizational innovation enable the technological innovation? The answer to both questions is probably yes. The history of biotechnology is a great example of the push and pull between technological innovation and organizational/institutional experimentation, or what Richard Nelson has called the "coevolution" of science, technology, and institutions.[1] In biotechnology, experimentation is not just occurring in the lab and the clinic, it is also happening in the board rooms, conference rooms, and all the other places where entrepreneurs, managers, venture capitalists, and others dream up new ways of doing business. The biotechnology industry has encapsulated thirty years of such experimentation, which have been explored in this book. This final chapter offers some reflections on the experiments, some speculations about the road ahead, and some suggestions about what needs to change to enable the sector to achieve its potential.

TAKING STOCK AND LOOKING AHEAD

A few basic conclusions can be drawn in taking stock of the biotech experiment. First, as a business, biotechnology has yet to realize its enormous commercial and economic potential. Only a very tiny fraction of new entrants have ever been profitable. In aggregate, the sector has lost money for a very long time. Even among the profitable firms, only a handful of "elites" have achieved substantial profits—and these were among the earliest entrants into the industry (Amgen, Genentech, Genzyme, Biogen, Idec, etc.). Perhaps only Amgen and Genentech can legitimately be considered to have broken into the league of established pharmaceutical companies—and Genentech is majority owned by the multinational pharmaceutical company Roche.

Second, there is no sign that biotechnology has revolutionized the productivity of pharmaceutical R&D, despite many long-standing claims to the contrary. R&D productivity continues to be a big problem for both established pharmaceutical companies and newer biotechnology entrants.

Finally, the sector appears to be retreating from its position at the radical and risky end of the R&D spectrum. It was supposed to be the entrepreneurial biotechnology firms, unshackled from tradition and bureaucracy, that would go where big pharmaceutical companies dared not. Unfortunately, the economics have not worked out, and biotechnology firms have moved from the frontier to less risky venues. There is, of course, nothing wrong with these strategies. Given the realities of private and public equity markets, they are perfectly reasonable and not surprising. And while many of these companies are not pushing the edge scientifically or searching for highly novel drugs to treat major diseases, they are doing valuable work. New formulations and refinements of existing molecules can lead to major therapeutic improvements and greatly expand treatment options. Nevertheless, this trend should give us pause. Entrepreneurial firms are expected to be at the cutting edge of research. If young biotech firms are not pursuing the high-risk strategies—if they are moving away from cutting-edge science—then who will focus on the higher-risk, long-term, and less scientifically mature projects that offer potential medical breakthroughs? Who will be on the vanguard of the biotechnology revolution in the future?

It is commonly argued in biotechnology that, given enough time, the sector will perform well. Projections of profitability being "just around the corner" have actually been made since the earliest days of the industry. Of course, like any prediction, these projections are hard to refute ex ante (but can certainly be validated ex post). To date, predictions of future economic health for biotech have been consistently wrong. While it is possible and plausible that economic health could come to biotech soon without any further structural changes, the arguments of the last chapter should make us cautious. More of the same strategy and structure is likely to lead to more of the same performance.

Another optimistic scenario that is commonly put forward can be summarized under the heading "technology saves the day": advances in the science—genomics, proteomics, systems biology, etc.—will make it possible to identify with a high degree of precision promising drug candidates at extremely early stages of the R&D process. This should lead to a dramatic reduction in uncertainty (i.e., attrition rates drop), R&D cycle times, and costs. A torrent of new drugs will be unleashed. Such a scenario would obviously entail a major upheaval in the economics of the drug industry and the biotechnology sector.

This scenario raises two questions. First, assuming the scenario pans out technologically, does it inevitably imply a positive economic picture for the industry? Much of the profitability of the drug business rests on the inherent uncertainty and risks of the R&D process. The risks create a barrier to entry; the low probabilities of success mean that there are few winners, but those that do win can generally do quite well. The profit picture of biotech reflects this economic logic: there are a few big winners (e.g., Amgen, Biogen-Idec, Genentech, Genzyme) but far more struggling enterprises. Technology and the accumulation of capabilities that reduce uncertainty will not necessarily lead to higher average profits (but they are likely to reduce the unevenness of the distribution).

The second question about this scenario concerns the transition path, namely, what should it look like? Even ardent optimists realize that the road to "technological nirvana" will be a long and tortuous one. Moreover, in order for the transition to happen, we need enterprises that can engage in and develop the basic science. We need organizations that can integrate the relevant technologies and bodies of knowledge, develop capabilities to generate, process, and utilize information, and learn (through trial and error) what works and what does not. In short, we need economically viable science-based enterprises.

What are the consequences of not being able to solve the business problems of the sector? Ultimately, poor economic performance—negative cash flows, low financial returns—are not sustainable from a business perspective. The sector will not be able to attract new investment and new talent. The great potential of biotech to transform health care will go unrealized.

The previous chapter looked at the contribution private enterprises could make to address the problems of the sector, focusing both on mind-sets and on appropriate organizational strategies and business models. Better strategies and better business models can help enormously, but they may not be enough. This chapter looks to the environment in which the firms operate. It includes the institutions of basic science (universities and the grants process), funding arrangements, and regulations. Each of these has a part to play in laying the foundation for a healthy biotechnology sector.

INSTITUTIONS OF BASIC SCIENCE

The institutions of basic science include academic research laboratories, government research institutes, and government funding of science. These institutions have played an important role in advancing the underlying sciences of biotechnology. It is hard to imagine what the life sciences would look like today without the National Institutes of Health, the University of California, Stanford, MIT, Columbia, University of Washington, Harvard, the Whitehead Institute, the Institute for Genomic Research, the Human Genome Project, the MRC Laboratory of Molecular Biology, dozens of academic medical centers, countless other governmental and academic laboratories around the world, and journals such as *Science* and *Nature*.

As noted in this book, these institutions are increasingly weaving together with the institutions of business, such as venture capital, patenting, and licensing and collaboration with for-profit enterprises. The links between the institutions of science and those of business are the subject of debate. A close connection between universities and private enterprise in the United States seems to play a critical role in the rapid commercialization of basic scientific knowledge. Indeed, in Europe, where both government policy and cultural norms have historically impeded tight university-industry relationships, there has been much discussion of emulating the "U.S. model" of academic entrepreneurship. Concerns expressed about the growing intimacy between universities and the private sector focus on the potential to subvert the "scientific commons" by converting publicly available scientific knowledge into private intellectual property.[2] In general, the evidence for deleterious effects of close university-industry relationships is mixed. While some survey research suggests that research agendas may be influenced by the prospects of commercial reward, there is little evidence that patenting, which is often associated with these latter activities and approaches, curtails dissemination of research findings through publication.[3]

Much of the debate about university activities in the business of science focuses on the impact of patents. In some ways, this debate focuses on the wrong question. It is not so much a matter of whether or not universities patent, but how they choose to use those patents and the extent to which they make the knowledge embedded in those patents broadly available. This book suggests one way to think about the issue. Innovation in biotechnology requires mechanisms for managing risk, integration, and learning. The question then is: How do the institutional arrangements of science and the links between these institutions and business influence the sector's capacity to manage risk, achieve integration, and facilitate learning? What changes may be beneficial along these dimensions?

Investments in basic science have the potential to increase the attractiveness of downstream R&D by reducing risks.[4] Advances in basic scientific knowledge (such as the invention of rDNA techniques or the creation of a map of the human genome) or the development of basic research tools (such as genomic sequencing or "knock-out" mice) lower the risks of more applied commercial development in two ways. First, they highlight directions where subsequent efforts may be fruitful (and likewise, flag less attractive paths). Lee Fleming and Olav Sorenson liken scientific advance to a map and scientific progress to a process of filling in the map's details.[5] Second, they provide researchers with tools for more rapidly and efficiently experimenting and thus generating information about attractive paths forward. We can think of basic research as generating information, which is the antidote to uncertainty, and thus to risk. In this sense, it is very straightforward to understand how scientific research might reduce R&D risks.

In order to have these beneficial effects on risk reduction, however, the information created by scientific research must be disseminated broadly. Any strategies or policies at the university level (such as exclusive licensing) that discourage or inhibit the broad flow of basic scientific information are clearly problematic. Using the Fleming-Sorenson analogy, a map given exclusively to one explorer simply does not have much impact if there are a hundred others wandering blindly. Even worse, in contexts like biotechnology, where basic scientific knowledge evolves with application of that knowledge to specific therapeutic problems, putting the science into the hands of more explorers is likely to accelerate the pace of scientific advance. Exclusive licensing (to an existing firm or to a start-up) may be appropriate for specific molecules with very specific therapeutic applications (e.g., a molecule that might suppress the growth of cancer cells) but is much less justified as we move upstream to more basic tools and techniques with many potential (but uncertain) paths for development.[6] Universities' taking equity positions in new firms would clearly seem to run counter to this.

Universities and the grants process have the potential to enhance R&D integration in two ways. First, they could create more integrated knowledge bases through interdisciplinary research. One of the barriers to integration in commercial R&D is that the knowledge base itself is fragmented into highly specialized niches. There is deep knowledge within specific disciplines (e.g., chemistry, genomics) but less knowledge that helps us understand connections across disciplines. Part of this is due to the organization of academic disciplines into highly specialized disciplines, each with its own set of local problems, language, intellectual goals, theories, accepted methods, publication outlets, and criteria for evaluating research. This is as true in the life sciences as it is in any other academic discipline. Part of the problem may also be due to the grants funding process, which tends to reward investigators for narrow, well-defined research projects. Like most systems, the grants process involves trade-offs. The current peer review process for grants is an excellent vehicle for quality control and for ensuring that decisions are based on scientific merit, but it can also create barriers to cross-disciplinary work (an issue discussed further below). Critics of the grants process point to the "war on cancer" as an example of how funding can divert researchers from the most important problems. According to one account, while metastatic processes lead to about 90 percent of all cancer deaths, less than 0.5 percent of National Cancer Institute study proposals made between 1972 and 2004 focused primarily on metastatis.[7]

One of the primary objectives of universities and the funding process in this space should be to reshape the scientific landscape through more integrated, cross-disciplinary research and training. There are already signs that this has begun to occur over the past decade, as universities have launched interdisciplinary institutes—such as the Broad Institute at Harvard and MIT—that bring together scientists from biology, chemistry, mathematics, computer science, physics, engineering, and medicine.

The second way universities influence integration is through their strategies and behaviors associated with new firm formation. University licensing strategy and policies toward new firm formation can have a powerful effect on the industrial landscape of biotechnology. And here again, we need to be suspect of exclusive arrangements that move IP into the hands of a single entity. That may well work to enhance integration if that entity has complementary technological and functional capabilities, but if the license goes to a start-up, that may exacerbate the problems associated with islands of expertise discussed in chapter 7.

There are three basic models of technology transfer, each of which is likely to be appropriate for different situations. At one extreme, we have the nonexclusive, "open" licensing of technology.

This does not necessarily mean free, but it does mean that technology is essentially available (on reasonable economic terms) for any entity that desires to take a license. This was the model that was used for the basic rDNA patents that drove the early formation of the biotechnology industry. This mode of transfer works best when the technologies in question represent broadly applicable tools, techniques, or concepts.

A second mode of technology transfer is exclusive licensing to an existing firm. Exclusivity is necessary when the technology in question is specific and when its value declines with access. So, for instance, a technology associated with a specific molecule, may be of great value to a firm that has a commercial interest in the disease(s) that might be treated with that molecule. However, the incentive to invest for further development is inhibited if the licensee faces other competitors. Licensing/collaboration with an existing firm is optimal when certain complementary assets, capabilities, and know-how are needed to fully exploit the technology in question. A novel cancer therapeutic, for example, might be more fully exploited if licensed to an organization with experience developing cancer drugs and designing and managing cancer clinical trials.

Finally, the start-up mode of technology transfer is likely to be optimal when the technology is so radically new that it is not complemented by existing technologies or organizational capabilities. For instance, highly novel therapeutic modes, like tissue engineering, might be better incubated inside a new firm that can build the essential capabilities from scratch.

The previous chapter admonished against the monetization mind-set of the biotechnology business community. Universities (faculty and administrators) might be similarly admonished. The monetization mind-set increasingly influences licensing and disclosure policies in ways that may inhibit the broad flow of critical scientific information. These policies are aimed at maximizing university licensing revenues and equity returns rather than maximizing the contribution to the scientific commons. A shift in mentality and policies is needed. Over the long term, the continued scientific advance of biotechnology and improving the prospects for commercially successful R&D requires greater emphasis on the scientific commons.[8]

FUNDING ARRANGEMENTS

As noted in previous chapters, pharmaceutical R&D, even in this age of advanced science, is characterized by profound and persistent uncertainty, a trait that challenges available funding models. Two basic problems must be solved. First, while government (in the United States) generously funds basic scientific research through such agencies as the NIH, and there is rich vein of venture capital available for new firms with more developed (less uncertain) product concepts, there is a gap in what is sometimes referred to as "translational research." Second, there are specific challenges associated with using public equity as a funding and governance model for biotechnology companies.

Crossing the Chasm: Translational Research

As the name implies, translational research translates basic scientific findings and concepts into specific product opportunities. While the definition is not precise and the boundaries are blurry, translational research bridges early-stage basic research and human clinical testing. For instance, research geared toward understanding how stem cells divide and become specialized cells would be an example of basic scientific research; developing hypotheses and insights about the clinical applications for treating diabetes would be examples of translational research. Cataloging the genetic mutations that cause normal cells to become cancerous would be an example of basic scientific research; developing hypotheses and identifying classes of compounds that might stop this process would be an example of translational research. Translational research encompasses activities such as target identification and validation, in vitro and in vivo screening, and perhaps some early-stage human clinical trials (Phase 1 or small-scale Phase 2).

Historically the problem with translational research is that it is in a sense "too applied" to attract funding from agencies such as the NIH that focus on basic scientific research. According to Keith Joiner, the grants process represents a major hurdle to conducting translational research:

There is a widely recognized tendency for review groups to fund well written applications for which the hypothesis being addressed is important, the preliminary data are compelling, but most importantly, the proposed experiments are likely to be successful and can be completed in the time frame of the award (personal observation). Direct applicability to human health may be discussed but rarely is used as an essential criteria in the funding decision . . . The complexities of conducting translational research, including insuring sufficient access to patients and volunteers, meeting regulatory challenges, conducting research in an only partially controlled setting, and dealing with expensive infrastructure, all preclude preparation of applications which have the crispness and apparent sophistication of more basic proposals.[9]

At the same time, translational research is increasingly considered too early (too risky, too long term) to attract private venture capital. Moreover, to undertake translational research requires investments in intellectual assets like novel animal models that may be difficult to commercialize or even protect.

There are two potential approaches for funding translational research. One is to consider extending the reach of government funding further downstream into translational research. This is already starting to happen with the NIH "Roadmap" and the creation of Director's Pioneer Awards to encourage investigators to tackle less explored, more risky areas of research.[10] There are examples of government funding playing a role in the nonbiomedical equivalent of translation research. For instance, the Defense Departments Advanced Research Project Agency (DARPA) has funded just this type of work in software, communications, computers, and electronics (including the prototype for the Internet).

A second approach comes from private-sector funding. This in itself can come in various forms. The largest pharmaceutical companies in the world may supply both the resources and the incentives to conduct some translational research on their own or in collaboration with universities. Novartis's Institute for Biomedical Research largely describes its mission as translational research. However, pure corporate R&D in this space does not get past the dissemination issues, although for translational work this may be less of a problem than for basic scientific research. Alternatively, consortia of companies may fund translational research programs at academic institutions.

An interesting and very promising alternative funding arrangement for translational research is venture philanthropy, which, as the name implies, is a hybrid institutional arrangement, combining elements of traditional not-for-profit philanthropy and traditional for-profit venture capital. Like a philanthropy, these organizations are privately funded (usually by wealthy individuals or families), not-for-profit entities, focused on a specific agenda. In the case of health care, venture philanthropy organizations have typically focused on advancing treatments for specific diseases. These organizations, however, approach the funding and management process very much along the lines of a traditional, for-profit venture capitalist. Funding is provided in stages, and milestone reviews are conducted. Venture philanthropists, like traditional venture capitalists, take a somewhat active approach in helping the recipients (by either providing management guidance or putting them in contact with other players in the network). Most importantly, venture philanthropists will fund private enterprises as well as academic researchers, usually receiving some type of (nonequity) return on their investment, which goes back into the foundation to provide additional funding.

Venture philanthropy is a relatively new organizational form. The Cystic Fibrosis Foundation, founded in 1955, is perhaps the oldest of this type. However, most venture philanthropy organizations have been founded in the past decade, including the Prostate Cancer Foundation (1993), the Institute for Aging (1998), the Multiple Myeloma Research Foundation (1998), the Bill and Melinda Gates Foundation for research on AIDS and infectious diseases in developing countries (2000), the Michael J. Fox Foundation for Parkinson's Research (2000), and Accelerate Brain Cancer Cure (2001).

Accelerate Brain Cancer Cure (ABC2) is typical of how such organizations operate. ABC2 focuses on moving potential compounds to treat brain cancer into human clinical testing. It not only funds the research but also takes an active role in organizing and managing the process. For instance, ABC2 funded Duke University's work to develop animal models for brain cancer and to establish a screening center. It then engaged a variety of private companies that had compounds in development for other cancers, and through a materials transfer agreement with Duke, had those compounds screened for activity against brain cancer. Companies working with ABC2 are provided access to the company network of academic and company collaborators. Under most circumstances, the originating company maintains the right to any compounds that show promise in early screening, with ABC2 receiving royalties on future sales.

It is too early to tell how venture philanthropy will impact biotechnology research. There are only a handful of such organizations, and the total funding is minuscule compared to the global universe of government and corporate R&D. And to date they have focused on only a handful of diseases. These organizations are also early in their missions, with years of effort in front of them to score major therapeutic breakthroughs. However, there are two features of venture philanthropy organizations that fit the requirements of the sector as outlined in this book. First, because of their funding structure, they have long time horizons. Their goal is to make a therapeutic difference, not to return a profit to limited partners in a three- to five-year period. This enables them to sustain highly uncertain investments over the requisite time frame. Second, they facilitate integration through proactive management of their network of collaborators. Most venture philanthropy organizations have some provisions for information sharing among collaborators (and indeed, some organizations make full information sharing a prerequisite for funding), and the organization itself can become a repository for shared learning.

Governance, Disclosure, and Financial Models

It has almost become a truism that the mark of success for a young entrepreneurial biotechnology firm is to go public. This should not be surprising. The act of going public enriches venture capital backers, founders, and employees of the firm, whose compensation is generally tilted toward options rather than salary. The paradox, of course, is that while going public is viewed as a badge of success, there are indeed precious few financially successful publicly held biotechnology firms (see chapter 6). We need to be careful in ascribing all the performance problems of biotechnology firms to their public equity governance structures; the causes of the biotechnology sector's performance problems are many and complex.

Nevertheless, there appears to be a mismatch between the challenges facing biotechnology firms and the properties of public equity governance. This mismatch is rooted in the fact that, for the vast majority of biotechnology firms, the value of the company depends heavily if not completely on in-process R&D projects. This raises two problems. One has to do with disclosure and valuation—essential ingredients for public equity markets to work efficiently. The other has to do with the long time horizon of the payoffs associated with most of these R&D projects. And these raise a third issue—is there a model that can provide the benefits of public equity without the downsides caused by these two problems?

Disclosure. One of the basic tenets of efficient capital markets is that information must be available to investors. For the vast majority of publicly traded companies in the economy, current disclosure rules, which focus heavily on financial parameters (like earnings), work reasonably well. For capital markets to work efficiently for science-based enterprises like biotechnology companies, disclosure frameworks that are better suited to the kinds of assets these companies possess are necessary.

Recent reforms, such as Sarbanes-Oxley (SOX) and Financial Accounting Standards Board Statements 141 and 142, increase disclosure burdens on all companies. With regard to intellectual property, companies face additional obligations to measure, monitor, and disclose the value of those assets and how material changes might impact financial performance.[11] While SOX and other reforms increase disclosure requirements, it is not clear they address particular issues of a science-based business like biotechnology. Throughout a development project, a company makes a myriad of technical decisions that influence the prospects and value of the project (e.g., the design of the clinical trial, interpretations of results). Under the current system, companies must disclose in a timely fashion the results of clinical trials that "materially impact" the prospects of the company. Ultimately, the final arbiter of whether a company has done a good job putting together the evidence to support the drug is the FDA or equivalent regulatory agency outside the United States.

In essence, the FDA acts very much like a third-party auditor that investigates the quality of the science and clinical data underlying the drug. (Of course, unlike financial auditors, the FDA is a government agency, not a for-profit enterprise paid by the client being audited.) It is a matter of much debate these days whether the FDA is doing a good job in this role. Some argue it is too lax, others argue it is too slow, others argue it is too tough. These issues aside, the biggest problem with FDA review, from an investor information point of view, is that it occurs largely at the end of the process, and much of the interchange between companies and the FDA throughout the process is private. The only other time the FDA is formally involved in the process in a public way is at the end of the process, when a company files its application for new drug approval or if it orders a halt of an ongoing clinical program based on safety concerns. It can advise companies on clinical designs or regulatory issues and concerns, but by and large it cannot mandate that a company execute its trials in a certain way. Nor does it interpret results for companies and make decisions about which drugs move into development (again, barring a serious safety concern). Those judgments lie with the company. And, as discussed in chapter 7, there is some evidence that those judgments are biased by the financial circumstances of the company and its alternative development options.

It may be that additional disclosure, focused on investor needs, is desirable earlier in the R&D process. Such suggestions are likely to be met with skepticism, if not downright hostility, from managers already feeling the burdens of SOX disclosure. However, research by Baruch Lev shows that increased disclosure of R&D actually has a positive effect on the market values of biotechnology companies.[12] This suggests that a regulatory solution is not actually needed, but that it is in companies' own interests to disclose more, not less, about their R&D projects.

Along these lines, an issue that needs to be seriously considered is greater disclosure of actual clinical trial data *during* the development process. This is clearly a controversial suggestion. Recently, in the wake of concerns over drug safety (and specifically the link between certain antidepressants and teen suicide), pharmaceutical companies have faced pressure to make public all clinical data for approved drugs. To date, such disclosures are voluntary, and there is no oversight of the process. In addition, the purpose of these disclosures is patient safety (and physician awareness), not investor appraisal. Making clinical data available during development is a complicated issue. On the one hand, it would certainly provide a high level of transparency; on the other hand, pharmaceutical companies rightly consider their clinical data to be extremely valuable and competitively proprietary.

There may be some intermediate solutions—for instance, reporting aggregate statistics. This is already done to some degree today through publication in peer review medical journals. However, which studies are submitted to a journal is completely at the discretion of a sponsoring drug company. This creates a bias in which only favorable results are published. In order for the information to be useful for investors, both positive and negative findings need to be made available, and they need to be made available early in the development process, not just after approval.

Obviously if full disclosure of clinical studies for the sake of patient safety and physician awareness is controversial, a call for disclosure of data early in the R&D process for investor information purposes is likely to encounter even more resistance. Ongoing clinical trials results are competitively valuable. An argument can be made that if companies are forced to disclose clinical data during the R&D process, the "free rider" problem will curtail their incentive to invest in R&D. This is a logical argument but represents only one half the trade-off. Making clinical data available earlier in the process could have two other benefits for pharmaceutical companies. First, better information for investors should lower the cost of capital. Right now, asymmetric information means that investors must discount the quality of information they receive from companies and essentially assign a higher-risk premium to their biotechnology investments. Second, even if competitors were able to exploit the information they learn about others' results, it is not entirely clear this would have a detrimental long-term effect. Competitors may learn about a promising approach, but they still need to do their own studies, and there is a significant time lag associated with this. In other words, there is still a strong first-mover advantage. In addition, making more information available would end up reducing uncertainty associated with drug R&D for all companies. Today companies make their R&D choices and clinical trial design decisions based largely on their own information, rather than on information about what has worked (and failed) for others. This inevitably must lead to wasted R&D effort as different companies essentially repeat the same errors. Fuller disclosure of clinical trial results may not only lead to better investment choices, but could also help with the R&D productivity problems facing the industry.

Rethinking the Publicly Held Biotech Firm. Even with much better disclosure, the concept of the publicly held biotechnology company can be questioned. A CEO of a publicly traded, profitable biotechnology firm we interviewed for this book confided (requesting anonymity), "I am just not sure the publicly traded biotechnology company is a viable model." He went on to explain that it was hard to run a business with ten-year investment cycles when facing short-term earnings pressure. Another CEO noted, "Here we are laying a financing model with a two- to three-year time window onto an industry with a twenty-year development cycle. It doesn't make sense." Of course, one could also argue the contrary, that given the extremely poor long-term performance of the biotechnology industry in general, and specific firms in particular, capital has been, if anything, too patient. Whether capital is too patient or too impatient, the result is the same: a misallocation of resources. Some firms may not get enough capital to fund truly important (and economically attractive) projects, while others may get too much capital to squander on questionable projects.

In considering alternative arrangements to publicly traded firms, it is necessary to first consider the properties of public equity that are indeed quite valuable. First, public equity provides access to major pools of capital, thus making it possible for companies to fund large-scale development efforts. Second, public equity markets are liquid and enable investors to diversify their risks. This not only lowers the cost of capital to firms, but also enables the funding of more risky ventures. Finally, the liquidity of public equity markets enables younger firms to attract scientific and management talent with stock options and other equity-based compensation schemes instead of cash compensation.

The Quasi-Public Corporation. There is a lot to like about public equity. But, as pointed out in chapter 7 and above, it does not quite fit the requirements of a science-based business like biotechnology. There are governance issues, disclosure issues, and time-horizon issues. Given these issues, *is there an institutional arrangement that enables us to keep the beneficial properties of public equity, without its inherent downside?* One possible alternative is the *quasi-public corporation*. As the name implies, these are entities that are publicly listed and publicly traded. Thus they follow all of the normal governance and disclosure rules of public corporations, and they have access to public equity markets. However, unlike normal public corporations, quasi-public entities have a majority of their stock held by a single entity with a long-term investment and strategic interest. That is, it is not just a financial relationship. Genentech actually fits this model, as 60 percent of its equity is owned by Hoffman-La Roche (and Roche's equity is 20 percent owned by Novartis).

Genentech's history is interesting because it illustrates the limits of the pure public model. After Genentech launched its third drug (tPA), it faced a significant gap in its product pipeline. This was due to the fact that the company had to spend most of its R&D resources on getting tPA through the development process. With few resources left to fund other projects, Genentech was in a difficult position after the launch of tPA. It had no prospective new products to launch for several years. And with tPA sales less than expected, it did not have the cash flow to reload its development pipeline. This led to an agreement with Swiss pharmaceutical giant Hoffman-La Roche in 1995 whereby Roche acquired a partial stake in Genentech and an option to acquire the remainder of the company within four years at a predetermined price that escalated quarterly (up to a preset maximum). The infusion of new capital at that point enabled Genentech to start a series of new R&D projects, including ones that eventually led to the launch of Herceptin and Avastin. In 1999 Roche exercised its option to acquire all remaining shares of Genentech. However, Roche announced almost immediately that it would sell back to the public approximately 19 percent of Genentech's stock. Genentech would maintain a separate board of directors (with three seats reserved for Roche representatives). The companies also agreed to a set of guiding principles for the relationship. Under these principles, Genentech would remain an independent operating entity. Over time, Roche gradually reduced its holdings by selling portions of its shares to the public. As of 2004, Roche held 56 percent of the outstanding shares of Genentech. Business dealings between Roche and Genentech operate under an arm's-length arrangement whereby Roche has certain rights to market Genentech products in Europe.

Genentech has obviously done extraordinarily well. It has been highly profitable; its R&D has been among the most productive in the industry having launched a series of medically important drugs. And despite its growth (it is clearly no longer a small company), Genentech has, by all accounts, maintained an entrepreneurial and science-oriented culture. The relationship between Genentech and Roche also appears to have worked well, and Genentech has been allowed to operate independently. We need to be careful not to ascribe all or even most of this success to its unusual governance structure. Genentech may have been just as successful under a variety of governance arrangements—it is always impossible to test a counterfactual hypothesis! In addition, because this arrangement is unusual, we do not have any kind of statistical base to assess whether firms operating under such majority ownership arrangements perform better than those that are not. In the vast majority of cases, established pharmaceutical companies have taken either very small equity stakes (less than 20 percent) in biotech partners or have opted for full acquisition.

Nevertheless, the example of the Genentech-Roche relationship at least offers an "existence proof" of the concept. If properly managed, such relationships might be a viable way to enable biotechnology companies to pursue longer terms R&D strategies, while providing the more intensive oversight of an informed investor. Of course, there is a fine line between informed oversight and meddling. One can easily imagine situations in which intensive oversight destroys the very entrepreneurialism and flexibility that was attractive to the larger partner in the first place. It has happened with a number of full acquisitions of biotechnology companies by large pharmaceutical companies. One of the advantages of keeping a significant portion of shares on the open market, and an independent board of directors, is that the arrangement establishes a fiduciary duty on the part of management and the board to act in the interests of all shareholders (not just the majority owner).

Like most organizational innovations, the quasi-public concept is not a panacea, nor is it appropriate for all companies. It would seem better suited to younger companies that need time and resources to develop their pipelines and initiate an earnings stream. At the same time, the target company needs to have sufficient technological and managerial capabilities already on board to be able to operate with sufficient independence. It is hard to ask the investing partner to keep a hands-off policy if the target entity is struggling. Indeed, Roche is widely given credit for letting Genentech operate independently, but this would have been a much harder policy to execute if Genentech had not been doing so well. The investing partner needs to have the discipline to allow the target company to operate independently (while exercising fiduciary oversight). And the investing partner needs to manage the compensation issue. If employees of the target company have stock options—the purpose of allowing the company's shares to trade publicly—then they could wind up with total compensation that dwarfs that of employees in the investing company. Such compensation differentials are an obvious source of tension and can lead relationships to sour. Thus the concept of a quasi-public biotechnology company is a structural solution to a governance problem, but it is not the total solution. Ultimately, running a science-based enterprise comes down to a set of management behaviors and approaches that may be quite different from those that work in most industry context.

TOWARD A SCIENCE-BASED ENTERPRISE

If we go back to one of the motivating questions of this book—Can science be a business?—it would appear that the answer, based on the experience to date, would be no. The business of science in biotechnology has not yet been profitable, nor has it been particularly productive in terms of turning scientific advances into drugs. This answer, however, is correct only if we take existing organizational and institutional arrangements and existing management technologies as given. What I have tried to show in this book is that science creates novel business requirements that cannot be fulfilled with these existing approaches. Organizational and institutional innovations are needed in order to unlock the potential of biotechnology. Major epochs of technological innovation have always been linked to transformational innovations in organizational forms and institutional arrangements. For example, about 150 years ago, the creation of rail and telegraph systems gave rise to the modern corporation, which separated ownership (shareholders) from (salaried) management. As Alfred Chandler has noted:

> The building and operating of rail and telegraph systems called for the creation of a new type of business enterprise. The massive investment required to construct those systems and the complexities of their operations brought the separation of ownership from management. The enlarged enterprises came to be operated by team of salaried managers who had little or no equity in the firm. The owners, numerous and scattered, were investors with neither the experience, the information, nor the time to make the myriad decision needed to maintain a constant flow of goods, passengers, and messages.[13]

Throughout the past century, the "modern" corporation has continued to evolve in concert with both technological innovation and institutional developments. The emergence of venture capital in the United States in the latter half of the twentieth century, for instance, gave rise to entrepreneurial organizations that played a key role in industries like semiconductors, software, computers, and communications.

Today we are in the midst of a similar transformation. Just as railroads and telegraphs needed the modern corporation and semiconductors and software needed venture capital, biotechnology needs enabling organizational and institutional innovations that together constitute the science-based enterprise. Thirty years into biotechnology, we are still learning what such science-based enterprises might look like, how they will work, and what kind of management skills will be needed to lead them. It is indeed a healthy sign that we have witnessed so much experimentation in biotechnology, despite the sector's struggles. Much has been learned, and much more will be learned. There is no more important challenge for both scholars and practitioners in twenty-first-century economies than contributing to our ever evolving knowledge of the business of science.

Appendix A

Biotechnology Companies Used in the Analyses of the Industry

Aaipharma
Aastrom Biosciences
Abgenix
Acadia Pharmaceuticals
Access Pharmaceuticals
Acusphere
Adolor
Advanced Viral Research
Advancis Pharmaceutical
ADVENTRX Pharmaceuticals
Aeolus Pharmaceuticals
Aeterna Zentaris
Affymetrix
Alexion Pharmaceuticals
Alfacell
Alkermes
Alliance Pharmaceutical
Allos Therapeutics

Alnylam Pharmaceuticals
Alteon
Amarin
Amgen
Amylin Pharmaceuticals
Anadys Pharmaceuticals
Anika Therapeutics
Antigenics
Aphton
Applera Celera Genomics
Arena Pharmaceuticals
Ariad Pharmaceuticals
ArQule
Array Biopharma
Aspreva Pharmaceuticals
AtheroGenics
Autoimmune Technologies
Auxilium Pharma

AVANIR Pharmaceuticals
AVANT Immunotherapeutics
Avax Technologies
AVI BioPharma
Avigen
Axcan Pharma
Axonyx
Barrier Therapeutics
BioCryst Pharmaceuticals
Biodelivery Sciences
    International
Bioenvision
Biogen
BioMarin Pharmaceutical
Biomira
Biopure
BioSante Pharmaceuticals
Biovail
Bone Care International
Boston Life Sciences
Caliper Life Sciences
CancerVax
Cardiome Pharma
Cardiovascular Biotherapeutic
Carrington Laboratories
Celgene
Cell Genesys
Cell Therapeutics
Cellegy Pharmaceuticals
CEL-SCI
Cephalon
Cerus Chiron
Cholestech
Ciphergen Biosystems
Collagenex Pharmaceuticals
Columbia Laboratories
Connetics

Corcept Therapeutics
Corgentech
Corixa
Cortech
Cortex Pharmaceuticals
CoTherix
Critical Therapeutics
Crucell
Cubist Pharmaceuticals
CuraGen
CV Therapeutics
Cygnus
Cypress Bioscience
Cytogen
Cytokinetics
CytRx
deCODE Genetics
Dendreon
Digene
Discovery Laboratories
Diversa
DORbiopharma
DOV Pharmaceutical
DUSA Pharmaceuticals
Dyax
Dynavax
Emisphere Technologies
Encysive Pharmaceuticals
Endovasc
EntreMed
Entropin
Enzo Biochem
Enzon Pharmaceuticals
Epimmune
Epix Pharmaceuticals
Ergo Science
EXegenics

Exelixis
Eyetech Pharmaceuticals
Favrille
Forbes Medi-Tech
Genaera
Genaissance Pharmaceuticals
Gene Logic
Genelabs Technologies
Genencor International
Genentech
Genitope Corp
Genta
GenVec
Genzyme
Geron
Gilead Sciences
GlycoGenesys
GTx
Guilford Pharmaceuticals
Helix BioMedix
Hemispherx Biopharma
Hemosol
Hollis-Eden Pharmaceuticals
Human Genome Sciences
Icagen
Icoria
ICOS
Idenix Pharmaceuticals
Illumina
ImClone
Imcor Pharmaceutical
Immtech International
Immune Response Corporation
ImmunoGen
Immunomedics
Incyte
Indevus Pharmaceuticals

Inhibitex
Inkine Pharmaceutical
Inspire Pharmaceuticals
Interferon Sciences
Interleukin Genetics
InterMune
IntraBiotics Pharmaceuticals
Introgen Therapeutics
Isis Pharmaceuticals
ISTA Pharmaceuticals
Iteration Energy
Keryx Biopharmaceuticals
Kos Pharmaceuticals
Kosan Biosciences
La Jolla Pharmaceutical
Large Scale Biology
Lexicon Genetics
Luminex
MacroChem
Manhattan Pharmaceuticals
Marshall Edwards
Martek Biosciences Corp
Matritech
Maxim Pharmaceuticals
Maxygen
Medarex
Medical Discoveries
The Medicines Company
MedImmune
Memory Pharmaceuticals
Metabasis Therapeutics
MGI PHARMA
Millennium Pharmaceuticals
Miravant Medical Technologies
Momenta Pharmaceuticals
Myogen
Myriad Genetics

Nabi Biopharmaceuticals
Nanogen
NatureWell
Nektar Therapeutics
NeoPharm
NeoRx
Nephros
Neurobiological Technologies
Neurocrine Biosciences
Neurogen
New River Pharmaceuticals
NitroMed
Northwest Biotherapeutics
Novavax
Noven Pharmaceuticals
Novogen
NPS Pharmaceuticals
Nuvelo
OccuLogix
Oncolytics Biotech
Onyx Pharmaceuticals
OraSure Technologies
Orchid Cellmark
Orphan Medical
Oscient Pharmaceuticals
OSI Pharmaceuticals
Osteotech
OXiGENE
Oxis International
Pain Therapeutics
Palatin Technologies
Peregrine Pharmaceuticals
Pharmacyclics
Pharmion
Pharmos
Point Therapeutics
Pozen

Praecis Pharmaceuticals
Progenics Pharmaceutical
Pro-Pharmaceuticals
Protein Design Labs
Provectus Pharmaceutical
QLT
Questcor Pharmaceuticals
Quidel
Regeneration Technologies
Regeneron Pharmaceutical
RegeneRx Biopharmaceuticals
Renovis
Repligen
Rigel Pharmaceuticals
Salix Pharmaceuticals
Sangamo BioSciences
Santarus
Savient Pharmaceuticals
SciClone Pharmaceuticals
Seattle Genetics
Senetek
Sepracor
Sequenom
SIGA Technologies
Sirna Therapeutics
SkyePharma
Sonus Pharmaceuticals
Spectrum Pharmaceuticals
Stellar Pharmaceuticals
StemCells
SuperGen
Synbiotics
Synthetech
Tanox
Tapestry Pharmaceuticals
Targacept-Redh
Targeted Genetics

Telik
Tercica
Theragenics
Theravance
Third Wave Technologies
Threshold Pharmaceuticals
Titan Pharmaceuticals
Transgene
Transgenomic
Transkaryotic Therapies
Trimeris
Trinity Biotech
Tripos
United Therapeutics
Valentis
Valera Pharmaceuticals
VasoActive Pharmaceuticals
Vernalis

Vertex Pharmaceuticals
ViaCell
Vical
Vicuron Pharmaceuticals
Vion Pharmaceuticals
Viragen
Viral Genetics
ViroLogic
ViroPharma
Vivus
Vyrex
Xcyte Therapies
Xenogen
Xenova Group
Xoma Ltd
Zila
Zonagen
ZymoGenetics

Appendix B

List of Pharmaceutical Companies Used in Productivity Analysis

Abbott Laboratories
Allergan
AstraZeneca
Aventis
Bayer
Bristol-Myers Squibb
Glaxo-Wellcome
Johnson & Johnson
Eli Lilly
Merck

Novartis
Novo Nordisk
Pfizer
Pharmacia & Upjohn
Rhone-Poulenc Rorer
Roche
Schering
Schering-Plough
SmithKline Beecham
Wyeth

Notes

Chapter 1

1. T. Agres, "Columbia Patents Under Attack," *The Scientist*, July 23, 2003, http://www.the-scientist.com/news/20030725/03.

2. J. West and M. Ashiya, "Technology Commercialization at the Massachusetts General Hospital," Case 9-604-090 (Boston: Harvard Business School Publishing, 2004).

3. On the cultural norms of science, the seminal work is R. K. Merton, "The Normative Structure of Science," in *The Sociology of Science: Theoretical and Empirical Investigations*, ed. N. W. Storer (Chicago: University of Chicago Press, 1973), 267–278.

4. R. R. Nelson, and S. G. Winter, "In Search of Useful Theory of Innovation," *Research Policy* 5 (1977): 36–76; G. Dosi, "Technological Paradigms and Technological Trajectories," *Research Policy* 11 (1982): 147–162. D. Sahal, "Technological Guideposts and Innovation," *Research Policy* 14 (1985): 61–82.

5. F. H. Knight, *Risk, Uncertainty and Profit* (Boston: Houghton Mifflin, 1921).

6. The National Cancer Institute, one of eight agencies part of the National Institute of Health, was allocated over $55 billion for funding cancer research from 1972 (following the initiation of President Nixon's "War on Cancer") through 2003.

7. See A. K. Klevorick et al., "On the Sources and Significance of Interindustry Differences in Technological Opportunities," *Research Policy* 24 (1995): 185–205, for a study of the mechanisms of appropriability in R&D.

8. See, for example, G. P. Pisano, R. Bohmer, and A. Edmondson, "Organizational Differences in Rates of Learning," *Management Science* 47, no. 6 (2001): 752–768.

Chapter 2

1. J. Drews, "Drug Discovery: A Historical Perspective," *Science* 287 (2000): 1960–1964.

2. A. A. J. Andermann, "Physicians, Fads, and Pharmaceuticals: A History of Aspirin," *McGill Journal of Medicine* 2, no. 2 (1996), http://www.mjm.mcgill.ca/issues/v02n02/aspirin.html.

3. A. Gambardella, *Science and Innovation: The U.S. Pharmaceutical Industry During the 1980s* (Cambridge: Cambridge University Press, 1995), 21.

4. H. A. Clymer, "The Economic and Regulatory Climate: U.S. and Overseas Trends," in *Drug Development and Marketing*, ed. R. B. Helms (Washington, DC: American Enterprise Institute, 1975), 138.

5. Drews, "Drug Discovery."

6. Two thousand of these molecules were studied by a chemist working for Pfizer, Christopher Lipinski, who found that: (1) in addition to their small size, most of these molecules contained fewer than ten nitrogen or oxygen atoms; (2) most of these molecules had five or fewer places in which a hydrogen atom was linked to an atom that was keen to get rid of the hydrogen atom; (3) most of these molecules were soluble in water and in fat. See "A Bigger Pill to Swallow," *The Economist*, September 6, 2001.

7. S. N. Cohen et al., "Construction of Biologically Functional Bacterial Plasmids in Vitro," *PNAS* 70, no. 11 (1973): 2340–2344.

8. So-called "over-expression" of a protein.

9. The first rDNA drug to be developed and approved for commercial use was recombinant insulin (developed collaboratively by Genentech and Eli Lilly) in 1982. Since that time, over sixty therapeutic proteins derived from rDNA have been developed and commercialized.

10. G. Köhler and C. Milstein, "Continuous Cultures of Fused Cells Secreting Antibody of Predefined Specificity," *Nature* 256 (1975): 495–497.

11. Polyclonal antibodies bind to the same protein but react with different parts of it.

12. These are cancerous cells providing immortality to the cell line by making it grow indefinitely.

13. R. C. Das, "Antibodies in Biotech's Year of the Bear," *American Biotechnology Laboratory*, May 2003, http://www.affitech.com/pdf/das4.pdf.

14. Stefan Thomke, *Experimentation Matters: Unlocking the Potential of New Technologies for Innovation* (Boston: Harvard Business School Press, 2003).

15. Aris Persidis, "Combinatorial Chemistry," *Nature Biotechnology* 18 (2000): IT50–IT52.

16. Drews, "Drug Discovery."

17. A. L. Hopkins and C. R. Groom, "The Druggable Genome," *Nature Reviews: Drug Discovery* 1 (2002): 727–730; K. Davies, "Cracking the 'Druggable Genome,'" *Bio IT World*, October 9, 2002, http://www.bio-itworld.com/archive; Drews, "Drug Discovery."

18. J. D. Watson, *DNA: The Secret of Life* (New York: Alfred A. Knopf, 2003), 63–64.

19. Prepared statement of J. Craig Venter before the Subcommittee on Energy and Environment, U.S. House of Representatives Committee of Science, Washington, DC, June 17, 1998.

20. The mouse genome was published in *Nature* in December 2002. Both mice and people have approximately thirty thousand genes, and 90 percent of the genes associated with inherited human diseases are also found in mice. Celera had sequenced the mouse genome a year earlier and made it available to customers for $15,000 per year. See "Science and Technology: Modest Mouse; Genomics," *The Economist* 365 (2002), 109.

21. Information from "Biotech's Billion Dollar Breakthrough," *Fortune*, May 26, 2003, 96–102; Sirna Therapeutics, Inc., http://www.sirna.com.

22. For an excellent and accessible overview of systems biology, see H. Kitano, "Systems Biology: A Brief Overview," *Science* 295 (2002): 1662–1664.

Chapter 3

1. This section contains information summarized from Rick Ng, *Drugs: From Discovery to Approval* (Hoboken, NJ: John Wiley & Sons, 2004).

2. These are sometimes referred to as Lipinski's "rule of five." Lipinsky et al. identified five characteristics of molecules that predict their likely success as a drug" (Lipinski et al., "Experimental and Computational Approaches to Estimate Solubility and Permeability in Drug Discovery and Development Settings," *Advanced Drug Delivery Review* 23, no. 3 [1997]: 3–25. See also M. MacCoss and T. A. Baillie, "Organic Chemistry in Drug Discovery," *Science* 303, no. 5665 [2004]: 1811).

Chapter 4

1. See *PAREXEL's Pharmaceutical R&D Statistics Book*, 2000.

2. J. A. DiMasi et al., "The Price of Innovation: New Estimates of Drug Development Costs," *Journal of Health Economics* 22 (2003): 151–185.

3. These statistics vary by therapeutic category, although the overall pattern is much the same. See J. A. DiMasi, "Risks in New Drug Development: Approval Success Rates for Investigational Drugs," *Clinical Pharmacology & Therapeutics* 69, no. 5 (May 2001): 301.

4. Baldwin and Clark define modularity as "a particular design structure, in which parameters and tasks are interdependent within units (modules) and independent across them." C. Y. Baldwin and K. B. Clark, *Design Rules*, vol. 1, *The Power of Modularity* (Cambridge, MA: MIT Press, 2000), 88.

5. Ibid.

6. D. J. Teece, *Strategy, Technology and Public Policy: Economists of the Twentieth Century* (Aldershot, UK: Edward Elgar, 1998); C. M. Christensen, *The Innovator's Dilemma: When New Technologies Cause Great Firms to Fail* (Boston: Harvard Business School Press, 1997); Baldwin and Clark, *Design Rules*.

7. See, for example, R. R. Nelson, and S. G. Winter, "In Search of Useful Theory of Innovation," *Research Policy* 5 (1977): 36–76; R. Nelson, "The Role of Knowledge in R&D Efficiency," *Quarterly Journal of Economics* 97, no. 3 (August 1982): 453–470; A. Gambardella, *Science and Innovation: The U.S. Pharmaceutical Industry During the 1980s* (Cambridge: Cambridge University Press, 1995); L. Fleming and O. Sorenson, "Science as a Map in Technological Search," *Strategic Management Journal* 25, nos. 8 and 9 (August–September 2004): 909–928.

8. R. Nelson, "The Role of Knowledge in R&D Efficiency"; A. Arora and A. Gambardella, "Evaluating Technological Information and Utilizing It: Scientific Knowledge, Technological Capability, and External Linkages in Biotechnology," *Journal of Economic Behavior and Organization* 24, no. 1 (1994): 91–114; A. Arora and A. Gambardella, "The Changing Technology of Technological Change: General and Abstract Knowledge and the Division of Innovative Labor," *Research Policy* 23 (1994): 523–532.

9. A. K. Pavlon and J. M. Reichert, "Recombinant Protein Therapeutics—Success Rates, Market Trends and Values to 2010," *Nature Biotechnology* 22, no. 12 (2004): 1513–1519.

10. T. G. Wolfsberg, J. McEntyre, and G. D. Schuler, "Guide to the Draft Human Genome," *Nature* 409 (February 15, 2001): 824–826.

11. Fleming and Sorenson, "Science as a Map in Technological Search."

12. J. Bogulavsky, "Target Validation: Finding a Needle in a Haystack," *Drug Discovery & Development* 5, no. 10 (November 2002): 41–48.

13. M. Iansiti, *Technological Integration: Making Critical Choices in a Turbulent World* (Boston: Harvard Business School Press, 1997).

14. T. S. Kuhn, *The Structure of Scientific Revolutions*, 2nd ed. (Chicago: University of Chicago Press, 1979).

15. G. Dosi, "Technological Paradigms and Technological Trajectories," *Research Policy* 11 (1982): 147–162.

16. See, for example, M. L. Tushman and P. Anderson, "Technological Discontinuities and Organizational Environments," *Administrative Science Quarterly* 31, no. 1 (1986): 439–465; R. M. Henderson and K. B. Clark, "Architectural Innovation: The Reconfiguration of Existing Product Technologies and the Failure of Established Firms," *Administrative Science Quarterly* 35, no. 1 (1990): 9–30; Christensen, *The Innovator's Dilemma*.

Chapter 5

1. http://www.gene.com.

2. This data is from firms that eventually went public. This caveat clearly introduces a "survivor bias" into our sample. However, the need to sample companies that filed an initial public offering was dictated by our goal of obtaining relatively detailed information about companies' technology strategies. When companies file their initial public offering registration statements, they are required to disclose very detailed information about their technology, their R&D projects in progress, and their overall technology strategy. Unfortunately, while it is possible to identify "biotechnology" companies that are privately held, there is no consistent detailed information available on these companies' technology strategies.

3. Genentech went public in 1980. Its initial offer price was $35/share, but its share price rocketed up to $88/share in less than one hour of being on the market. This was, at the time, one of the largest daily stock price increases of a newly public firm in its first day of trading.

4. M. McKelvey, *Evolutionary Innovations: The Business of Biotechnology* (Oxford: Oxford University Press. 1996), 105.

5. Tufts estimated cost of developing a new drug in 1970s to be approximately $300 million. See R. W. Hansen, "The Pharmaceutical Development Process: Estimates of Current Development Costs and Time and the Effects of Regulatory Change," in *Issues in Pharmaceutical Economics*, ed. R. I. Chien (Lexington, MA: Lexington Books, 1979), 151–187.

6. Information obtained from Genentech 10-K SEC report, December 31, 1980.

7. Ibid.

8. G. P. Pisano and P. Y. Mang, "Manufacturing, Firm Boundaries, and the Protection of Intellectual Property," working paper 92-048, Harvard Business School, 1992.

9. Clifton Leaf, "Why We're Losing the War on Cancer and How to Win It," *Fortune*, March 22, 2004: 76–97.

10. Cetus, for instance, bet its existence on getting Il-2 to market as a treatment for cancer. When the FDA failed to approve the drug the company was forced to sell itself to its Emeryville neighbor, Chiron.

11. P. Landers, "Drug Industry's Big Push into Technology Falls Short: Testing Machines Were Built to Streamline Research but May Be Shifting," *Wall Street Journal*, February 24, 2004.

12. J. Sorensen and T. Stuart, "Aging, Obsolescence, and Organizational Innovation," *Administrative Science Quarterly* 45 (2000): 81–112.

13. R. Henderson and I. Cockburn, "Scale, Scope and Spillovers: The Determinants of Research Productivity in Drug Discovery," *Rand Journal of Economics* 26, no. 1 (1996): 32–59.

14. Novartis, for instance, moved its research headquarters from Basel, Switzerland, to Cambridge, Mass., in order to be closer to "ground zero" of the genomics revolution. They hired Mark Fishman, a former Harvard Medical School professor and Massachusetts General Hospital physician, and an expert on genetics, to head up research. Merck hired Peter Kim, formerly at the Whitehead Institute—a leading center of genomic research. Merck and Pfizer also created research operations in the Boston area.

15. Pharmaceutical Research and Manufacturers of America (2002), reported in *PAREXEL's Pharmaceutical R&D Statistics Book*, 2003/04, 9.

16. Based on analysis of R&D pipelines contained in *PAREXEL's Pharmaceutical R&D Statistics Book*, 2002.

17. I. Guedj, "Ownership vs. Contract: How Vertical Integration Affects Investment Decisions in Pharmaceutical R&D," unpublished manuscript, November 24, 2004.

18. Office of Technology Assessment, Congress of the United States, *Commercial Biotechnology: An International Analysis* (Washington, DC: U.S. Government Printing Office, 1984).

19. See Research and Markets report entitled "Strategies for Innovation in Pharmaceutical R&D: Enhancing R&D Through Biotech Alliances and CRO Outsourcing". The summary is available at http://www.researchandmarkets .com/reports/c16797/. See also P. McGee, "Virtual Discovery and Development; Partnerships and Licensing Compounds Help TAP Transform Research and Development into Search and Development," *Drug Discovery and Development* (June 1, 2005): 26.

20. D. Leonard-Barton and G. P. Pisano, "Monsanto's March into Biotechnology (A)," Case 9-690-009 (Boston: Harvard Business School Publishing, 1990).

21. J. Lerner and R. P. Merges, "The Control of Technology Alliances: An Empirical Analysis of the Biotechnology Industry," *Journal of Industrial Economics* 46, no. 2 (1998): 125–156.

Chapter 6

1. G. S. Burrill, "Biotech 2002: The 16th Annual Report on the Industry" (San Francisco: Burrill, 2002), 289.

2. Data analysis from Stelios Papadopulos (S. G. Cowen), Ibbotson Associates, and Brinnyl Associates, and the *Wall Street Journal*. See D. B. Hamilton, "Biotech's Dismal Bottom Line," *Wall Street Journal*, May 20, 2004, 1.

3. "US Venture Capital Returns Remain Negative but Outperform Public Markets," *Venture Economics*, October 16, 2001.

4. R. Mullin, "Biotech Vies for Position," *Chemical and Engineering News* 81, no. 4 (January 27, 2003): 27–40.

5. G. Ashton and F. Kermani, "Getting to Grips with Attrition Rates," *CMR News* 20, no. 1 (2002): 8–9.

6. www.pharmaprojects.com.

7. "Resolving Anticompetitive Concerns, FTC Clears $16 Billion Acquisition of Immunex Corp. by Amgen Inc. (for release: July 12, 2002)," http://www.ftc.gov/opa/2002/07/amgen.htm.

Chapter 7

1. L. G. Zucker, M. R. Darby, and M. B. Brewer, "Intellectual Human Capital and the Birth of U.S. Biotechnology Enterprises," *American Economic Review* 88, no. 1 (March 1998): 290–306.

2. Powell et al. also show that strong local venture capital and other local conditions play a complementary role in shaping the location of new biotech firm formation (W. Powell et al., "The Spatial Clustering of Science and Capital: Accounting for Biotech Firm-Venture Capital Relationships," *Journal of Regional Studies* 36, no.3 [2002]: 291–305).

3. C. Menapace, "The Best Biotech Location," *Business Facilities* (April 2002), http://www.facilitycity.com/busfac/bf_02_04_special2.asp.

4. P. Kelley, W. K. Bunker, and W. W. Powell, "The Institutional Embeddedness of High-Tech Regions: Relational Foundations of the Boston Biotechnology Community," in *Clusters, Networks, and Innovation*, ed. S. Breschi and F. Malerba (Oxford: Oxford University Press, 2005), 262–296.

5. M. Edwards, "The Equity of Equity: Academic Profits from Life Science IPOs," Presentation to the Institute of Medicine, 35th Anniversary Annual Meeting, 2005.

6. M. McKelvey, *Evolutionary Innovations: The Business of Biotechnology* (Oxford: Oxford University Press, 1996), 132.

7. P. A. Gompers, "Contracting and Control in Venture Capital," Case no. 9-298-067 (Boston: Harvard Business School Publishing, 1998).

8. Ibid.

9. S. Kortum and J. Lerner, "Assessing the Contribution of Venture Capital to Innovation," *Rand Journal of Economics* 31, no.4 (2000): 674–692; P. Gompers and J. Lerner, "The Venture Capital Revolution," *Journal of Economic Perspectives* 15, no 2 (2001): 145–168.

10. Thomson Financial, VentureExpert database.

11. S. Nicholson, P. Danzon, and J. McCullough, "Biotech-Pharma Alliances as a Signal of Asset and Firm Quality," *Journal of Business* (forthcoming).

12. M. McCully, "Current Trends in Deals and Financing, Recombinant Capital," presented at GTCbio's Metabolic Diseases World Summit, Partnering and Deal-Making, July 1, 2005, available at rDNA.com.

13. B. Lev, "Sharpening the Intangibles Edge," *Harvard Business Review*, June 2004, 108–116; R. Guo, B. Lev, and N. Zhou, "Competitive Costs of Disclosure by Biotech IPOs," *Journal of Accounting Research* 42, no. 2 (May 2004): 319–355.

14. I. Guedj and D. Scharfstein, "Organizational Form and Investment: Evidence from Drug Development Strategies of Biopharmaceutical Firms," NBER working paper 10933, Cambridge, MA, March 2004.

15. I. Guedj, "Ownership vs. Contract: How Vertical Integration Affects Investment Decisions in Pharmaceutical R&D" (unpublished manuscript, MIT Sloan School of Management, 2004).

16. A. Pollack, "Is Biotechnology Losing Its Nerve?" *New York Times*, February 29, 2004.

17. S. Heuser, "Boston Scientific May Pay $750m to Settle Stent Fight," *Boston Globe*, August 17, 2005.

18. A. Edmondson, et al., "Learning How and Learning What: Effects of Tacit and Codified Knowledge on Performance Improvement Following Technology Adoption," *Decision Sciences* 34, no. 2 (2003): 197–223.

Chapter 8

1. D. J. Teece, *Strategy, Technology and Public Policy: Economists of the Twentieth Century* (Aldershot, UK: Edward Elgar, 1998); D. J. Teece, "The Market for Know-how and the Efficient International Transfer of Technology," *Annals of the Academy of Political and Social Science* 4, no. 58 (November 1981): 81–96; D. J. Teece, "Transaction Cost Economics and the Multinational Enterprise: An Assessment," *Journal of Economic Behavior and Organization* 7 (1986): 21–45; G. P. Pisano, "The Governance of Innovation: Vertical Integration and Collaborative Arrangements in the Biotechnology Industry," *Research Policy* 20 (June 1991): 237–249; G. P. Pisano, "Using Equity Participation to Support Exchange: Evidence from the Biotechnology Industry," *Journal of Law, Economics and Organization* 5, no. 1 (Spring 1989): 109–126; A. Arora, A. Fosfuri, and A. Gambardella, "Markets for Technology and Their Implications for Corporate Strategy," *Industrial and Corporate Change* 10, no. 2 (2001): 419–451.

2. D. J. Teece, *The Multinational Corporation and the Resource Costs of Technology Transfer* (New York: Ballinger Publishing Company, 1976).

3. J. Lerner and U. Malmendier, "Contractibility and Contract Design in Strategic Alliances," working paper 11292, National Bureau of Economic

Research, Cambridge, MA, December 2004. For a sample of 584 research agreements struck between 1980 and 2001, they find an average contract duration for research alliances to be 3.9 years.

Chapter 9

1. R. R. Nelson, *Technology, Institutions, and Economic Growth* (Cambridge, MA: Harvard University Press, 2005).

2. M. Heller and R. Eisenberg, "Can Patents Deter Innovation? The Anticommons in Biomedical Research," *Science* 280 (May 1998): 698–701; Nelson, *Technology, Institutions, and Economic Growth*, chap. 9.

3. For a review of these studies, see P. Azoulay, W. Ding, and T. Stuart, "The Impact of Academic Patenting on (Public) Research Output," unpublished manuscript, Columbia University, July 15, 2004.

4. On the role basic scientific research in stimulating R&D productivity, see R. Nelson, "The Role of Knowledge in R&D Efficiency," *Quarterly Journal of Economics* 97, no. 3 (August 1982): 453–470.

5. L. Fleming and O. Sorenson, "Science as a Map in Technological Search," *Strategic Management Journal* 25, nos. 8 and 9 (August–September 2004): 909–928.

6. Nelson, *Technology, Institutions, and Economic Growth*.

7. C. Leaf, "Why We're Losing the War on Cancer and How to Win It," *Fortune*, March 22, 2004, 77–92.

8. An elegant statement of these issues, and an argument I have found very persuasive, can be found in Nelson, *Technology, Institutions, and Economic Growth*, chapters 8 and 9.

9. K. A. Joiner, "The Not-for-Profit Form and Translational Research: Kerr Revisited?" *Journal of Translational Medicine* 3, no. 19 (2005), http://bmc.ub.uni-potsdam.de/1479-5876-3-19/.

10. Division of Strategic Coordination, OPSAI, "NIH Roadmap for Medical Research," http://nihroadmap.nih.gov/overview.asp.

11. L. Vertinsky, "Expanded Role of IP Audits in the Aftermath of Sarbanes-Oxley," *IP Newswire*, November 2003, http://www.ipnewswire.com/articles/sox_audit.html.

12. B. Lev, "Sharpening the Intangibles Edge," *Harvard Business Review* (June 2004): 108–116.

13. A. D. Chandler, *Scale and Scope: The Dynamics of Industrial Capitalism.* (Cambridge, MA: Belknap/Harvard University Press, 1990), 1.

Index

About the Author

Gary P. Pisano is the Harry E. Figgie, Jr. Professor of Business Administration at the Harvard Business School, where he serves as head of the Technology and Operations Management Unit. For the past twenty years, his research has focused heavily on issues of technology strategy and the management of product and process innovation in biotechnology, pharmaceuticals, and health care. He is the author of *The Development Factory*, a book investigating the strategies and practices leading to superior development performance in biotechnology and pharmaceuticals. At Harvard Business School, Professor Pisano has taught MBA and executive courses in strategy, technology and operations management, and product development. In addition to his teaching and research, Professor Pisano has served as an adviser to senior executives at a number of companies in pharmaceuticals, biotechnology, and other technology-intensive businesses. Professor Pisano holds a PhD from the University of California, Berkeley and a BA in economics from Yale University.